Deflationism and Semantic Theories of Truth

Michael K Butler

Published by:
Pendlebury Press Limited
20 May Road
Swinton, Manchester M20 5FR
United Kingdom

ISBN: 978-0-9935945-4-0

"The semantical paradoxes are sometimes dismissed as mere curiosities, brain-teasers that amuse the technically minded but need not trouble those with deeper philosophical concerns. This complacency has always surprised me. I should have thought that, inasmuch as no notion is more central to philosophy than the notion of truth, the fact that we are unable to give even the rudiments of a consistent theory of truth for our own language would have been a cause for some alarm."

Vann McGee,

Truth, Vagueness, and Paradox,

Hackett (1991)

CONTENTS

ACKNOWLEDGMENTS

I would like to thank Jeffrey Ketland for many valuable discussions via email during 2000 and 2001, without which this work could not have been completed.

I would also like to thank my publisher, Geoffrey Howard of Pendlebury Press, for encouraging me to publish this work.

INTRODUCTION

One of the most important debates about truth in the last hundred years has been, ironically, whether or not truth is a worthy subject for philosophical debate at all. On the one hand, some philosophers have tried to give substantive accounts of truth, via theories of pragmatism, coherence, and correspondence. However, none of these has provided an account that has gained general acceptance. Indeed, many are of the opinion that such theories have been dismal failures. In the wake of difficulties encountered, many have turned to deflationary accounts of truth. These are often motivated by the *transparency* property of the truth predicate. The assertion "'Caesar was murdered' is true" is materially equivalent to the assertion "Caesar was murdered". Indeed, the two might be regarded as synonymous. Because of this it has been suggested that, despite appearances to the contrary, truth is a notion lacking in content and therefore not a worthy subject for philosophical analysis. The reason why attempts at such analysis have failed, so the argument runs, is that *there is no content to analyse.* The suggestion is that the ordinary intuition of truth that might be expressed by the *equivalence schema*

$$\text{'}p\text{' is true if and only if } p$$

exhausts all that may be said about truth.

The main purpose of the present work is to present some observations by Jeffrey Ketland in the broader context of the debate between substantive and deflationary theories of truth. Ketland's paper, *Deflationism and Tarski's Paradise* [16], attempts to show that deflationary accounts of truth are inadequate by demonstrating certain formal properties of Tarski's theory of truth. In the abstract he states "various deflationary theories behave somewhat differently to the standard Tarskian truth theory. These results suggest that Tarskian theories of truth are not redundant or dispensable."

Similar observations were made by Stewart Shapiro the previous year in *Truth and Proof: Through Thick and Thin* [28]. Ketland notes that deflationism is a very broad church, and Shapiro declares that "there are as many - or more - versions of deflationism as there are deflationists." It follows that in order to evaluate Ketland's degree of success we need to isolate precisely which features of deflationary theories he is arguing against.

Accordingly, Chapter 1 begins by reviewing the debate between *substantive* theories, according to which truth is a notion of philosophical significance, and *deflationary* theories that deny this.

Next, we introduce the best known of the *semantic paradoxes*, that of the *liar*. The liar sentence says of itself that it is false. This self-reference produces the well known phenomenon whereby whatever

11

truth-value we assign to the sentence, logical argument always results in the assignment of the opposite value, leading to a contradiction. Various attempts to resolve this paradox are discussed, in particular the language levels approach of Alfred Tarski.

Much of Ketland's paper is quite technical in character. Appreciation of the arguments therein requires familiarity with the essential features of formalised languages, in particular predicate calculus, and the broad significance of the Incompleteness Theorems of Kurt Gödel. This technical background is presented, without philosophical analysis, in Chapter 2.

In 1933 Alfred Tarski published in Polish the first edition of his paper *The Concept of Truth in Formalised Languages*, an English translation of which is reprinted in [33]. His stated aim in this work was, "to construct a materially adequate and formally correct definition of the term 'true sentence'". Tarski's initial paper contains the full technical description of his results. Two follow-up papers, [30] and [31], give a less technical discussion of his theory, and answer some of the criticisms that it received. Mindful that Tarski's work has often been misunderstood, I am careful here to present an accurate description of his theory. This is the purpose of Chapter 3.

In Chapter 4 we review some of Ketland's work. We begin by introducing the property of *conservativeness*. We may extend a given theory by adding further axioms, in particular those of a theory of truth. If the extended theory has no theorems that were not already theorems prior to extension, we say that the extension is *conservative*. By formalising certain well-known deflationary theories of truth, Ketland uses model-theoretic methods to show that such theories produce conservative extensions. By contrast, he demonstrates that Tarski's theory may produce an extension that is *not* conservative. It follows that Tarski's theory is richer than its deflationary rivals, in the sense that it enables us to derive results that cannot be derived via deflationary theories.

Tarski's language-level approach to resolving the semantic paradoxes is similar in some respects to the theory of types that Bertrand Russell advanced to resolve the paradoxes in set theory. However, Russell's theory of types has since largely been supplanted by type-free set theories. These resolve the paradoxes without recourse to infinite hierarchies of different types of entity. In view of this, it seems anomalous that Tarski's approach should be preferred in resolving the semantic paradoxes.

In Chapter 5 we examine an early type-free theory of truth, devised by Saul Kripke [19]. This allows certain sentences to be neither true nor false so that they *lack* truth value. We uncover some misconceptions about such theories in the literature on truth, and suggest that these provide a viable alternative to the Tarskian approach.

1
THEORIES OF TRUTH AND THE LIAR PARADOX

1.1 The Problem of Truth

From ancient to modern times philosophers have been perplexed by what is sometimes referred to as *the problem of truth*. Questions such as "What is the meaning of truth?", "How ought truth be defined?" and even "What is truth?" have produced a bewildering array of disparate suggestions and theories, with much dispute ensuing. One source of the difficulty is that it has seldom been articulated just what this *problem of truth* is supposed to be. Indeed, examination of the theories offered suggests that there is no single problem that all attempt to solve. Different theories have been advanced in attempts to answer quite different questions, or to solve quite different problems. Richard Kirkham observes that not only is this the case, but that often the writers concerned fail to discern that a theory of a perceived opponent is intended to solve a different problem from that tackled by their own theory [18]. Accordingly, I begin by reviewing Kirkham's distinction between three projects concerned with truth. In my description of these I adhere to his terminology.

Another point on which writers on truth diverge is as to what sort of entities are supposed to be true or false. Candidates for the *truth bearers* have included linguistic entities, in particular sentences, psychological entities such as thoughts or beliefs, abstract entities such as propositions or statements, and on rare occasion people and objects ("He was a true friend", etc.). For the sake of simplicity in what follows I shall take sentences as the truth bearers.

The *metaphysical project* aims to give necessary and sufficient conditions for a given sentence to be true. That is, it attempts to fill in the blank in a schema of the form

$$S \text{ is true iff } .....$$

where 'iff' abbreviates 'if and only if'. Some theories that have been proposed are, roughly:

Pragmatism: S is true iff it is useful to believe S.

Coherence: S is true iff S is consistent with accepted truths

Correspondence: S is true iff S corresponds to a fact.

By contrast, the *speech act project* attempts to elucidate *what we are saying* when we assert a sentence as true. Hence, this project attempts to provide *synonyms* for assertions of the form

$$S \text{ is true}$$

For example, one might maintain that in asserting the truth of a sentence one is merely agreeing with it, so that an appropriate synonym is

the speaker agrees with S.

Finally we mention the *justification project*. This is not an attempt to provide a theory of truth at all, although it has frequently been confused with such projects. It is concerned with what conditions need to be met in order that one might *reasonably accept* a sentence as true, rather than with what it actually *is* for that sentence to be true. The prevalence of *psychologism* in the late nineteenth century which favoured psychological explanations of many notions, including truth, may have led to the misclassification of some theories of justification as theories of truth. Frege makes the point well:

> "Being true is different from being taken to be true, whether by one or many or everybody, and in no case is to be reduced to it. There is no contradiction in something's being true which everybody takes to be false. I understand by 'laws of logic' not psychological laws of takings-to-be-true, but laws of truth. If it is true that I am writing this in my chamber on the 13th of July, 1893, while the wind howls out-of-doors, then it remains true even if all men should subsequently take it to be false. If being true is thus independent of being acknowledged by somebody or other, then the laws of truth are not psychological laws: they

are boundary stones set in an eternal foundation, which our thought can overflow, but never displace." [11]

Since in this present work we are concerned with being true rather than being taken-to-be-true, we shall not be concerned with the justification project. However, we include it here to ensure that the error of confusing justification with truth is guarded against.

1.2 Correspondence Theories

An ongoing debate which began early in the twentieth century concerns whether or not *truth* is concept of any deep philosophical significance. On one side of the debate, those who believe that truth is a substantial concept have attempted to provide an analysis of truth. Perhaps the most compelling family of substantive theories are the *correspondence theories*. According to such theories truth is a language-world relation, so that a sentence or other truth bearer is *true* when it accords with how things actually are. Each truth corresponds to some worldly relata, such as a *fact* or a *state of affairs that obtains.* Hence correspondence theories usually instantiate the metaphysical project by providing a schema of the form

S is true iff *S* corresponds to *X* and *X* obtains

for each sentence name *S*. *X* is the worldly correlate of the given true sentence, sometimes called its *truthmaker.* Individual theories have varied as to what they take as the truth bearers, the truthmakers, and the precise nature of correspondence. Bertrand Russell for example takes beliefs as truth bearers and understands correspondence as *congruence* [26]. In correspondence as congruence the individual elements of the belief mirror the individual elements of the correlated fact. Thus, a belief that *the cat sits on the mat* has constituents of cat, mat, and the relation of sitting that are mirrored in the corresponding fact. By contrast, J. L. Austin takes propositions as truth bearers and understands correspondence as *correlation*:

> "We are absolutely free to appoint *any* symbol to describe *any* type of situation, so far as

merely being true goes. There is no need whatsoever for the words used in making a true statement to 'mirror' in any way, however indirect, any feature whatsoever of the situation or event." [1]

In correspondence as correlation, it is the *whole* proposition that is to be correlated with the corresponding fact.

Correspondence fulfils the metaphysical project in a manner that accords well with common sense: a sentence is true if and only if it corresponds to a fact. However, some believe that this is merely empty paraphrasing, for example Crispin Wright:

"This piece of common sense is not to be confused with the idea that, understood one way, correspondence is nothing more than a platitude. The platitude is that predications of 'true' may always harmlessly be glossed in terms of correspondence to fact, telling it like it is, etc. These paraphrases incorporate no substantial commitment about the structure of truth." [34] page 208.

Some considerable difficulties are met by correspondence theories. In particular, the precise nature of the truthmakers is obscure. Even granted that 'the moon is spherical' is made true by the existence of a corresponding truthmaker, namely a spherical moon, of what does this fact consist? Presumably the fact comprises an individual, that is the moon, and a property of being spherical. However, it is clear that both the moon and spherical things might exist without yet the moon being spherical.

Also, there is no obvious truthmaker for the following sentence

the moon is not cube-shaped

Here it is the non-existence of a cube-shaped moon that makes the sentence true. Even more problematic is

if the moon was cube-shaped,

then it would have eight corners.

Since any cube has eight corners we would wish to admit this as true. However, there is no obvious candidate for the truthmaker for such a sentence.

By employing such lines of argument Julian Dodd has urged that *facts* should not be taken as entities that exist in the world. For a proposition that asserts the content of *"a* is *F"* where *a* is an individual and *F* a property, we may concede that *a* exists and we may even concede that *F* exists, but there is no existing *fact* of *a being F*. Dodd proceeds to argue for the identification of *facts* with *true thoughts*. It follows that the supposed correspondence of such theories is nothing more than *identity*. The facts that we supposed to be the truthmakers, are actually the truth bearers themselves:

> "If we take propositions to be thoughts [...] we seem to have the opportunity to wield Occam's Razor and identify facts with true thoughts. The mistake made by the correspondence theorist is that of taking facts to be truthmakers instead of true thoughts." [6] page 6.

Whilst granting that the ontological status of facts is problematic, the identity theory of truth seems to me to leave language divorced from reality. If indeed there are no objective truthmakers for true sentences, then it appears that truth does not depend at all upon the way that the world is. This is point is made most starkly by considering sentences that are even more basic than those of the object-predicate type, namely simple assertions of existence. Consider

the moon exists.

Surely the truthmaker for this sentence is the moon itself. Are we, on Dodd's view, to identify the truthmaker of this sentence with the *true thought* that the moon exists? This seems to me a poor candidate for truthmaker compared to the moon itself, existing as a mind independent body. Dodd acknowledges this difficulty himself, albeit in a footnote:

> "Actually, this is a little quick, for we can find truthmakers for certain truths without having to populate the world with proposition-shaped entities. <Susan exists> and <Susan=Susan> both need only Susan herself to exist in order to be true. None the less, for the overwhelming majority of truths it looks as though we will have to introduce more exotic entities to play

the truthmaking role." [6] note on page 17.

It is not our purpose to decide this debate here. It suffices to say that the difficulties faced in sustaining a correspondence view have caused many to turn to *deflationary* accounts of truth. These are the subject of the next section.

1.3 Deflationism: Redundancy, Disquotation, and Minimalism

We now turn to the other side of the debate about truth, according to which truth is not a substantive notion. This school of thought has become known as *deflationism* about truth. The theories that have been brought under the umbrella of deflationism exhibit a range of different features, but share a conviction that, "The correspondence theory, pragmatism, and coherence make truth a lofty matter. Deflationism makes it a trivial one." [27]

An early deflationary theory was proposed by Frank Ramsey, who believed that

"There is really no separate problem of truth but merely a linguistic muddle. It is evident that 'It is true that Caesar was murdered' *means no more* than Caesar was murdered, and 'It is false that Caesar was murdered' *means* that Caesar was not murdered." [25] (italics mine)

On this view, a suitable synonym for

it is true that *p*

is simply the sentence *p*. Attributing truth to *p* adds nothing to what is expressed by *p* alone, and hence is *redundant*. Since Ramsey was concerned with what it *means* to *say* that a sentence *p* is true, the redundancy theory is attempting to fulfil the speech-act project. Of course, although truth might be redundant in making assertions of the form 'it is true that *p*', it still finds its use in making indirect assertions ("What Tarski just said is true") and compendious assertions ("All that Kripke says is true"), and this is frequently held to be the reason why our language contains a notion of truth.

Kirkham points out that one can subscribe to redundancy without being a deflationist in this sense;

one can believe that 'is true' is redundant in various contexts but nevertheless maintain that truth *is* a genuine predicate. Conversely, one might hold that truth is not a genuine predicate, but nevertheless concede that truth still has a *use* and hence is not redundant.

> "One could hold, for example, that 'is true' is sometimes used to name a property and othertimes used merely to signal agreement, assert something in a stylish way, [etc.] Alternatively, one could hold that 'is true' always, or at least sometimes, names a property and signals agreement (asserts something in a stylish way, etc.). For that matter one could hold that truth is a property but the human predicament is such that we never need to refer to that property with a predicate and thus 'is true' is *only* used to signal agreement (assert in a stylish way, etc.). The latter position would be implausible but not logically inconsistent." [18], page 330.

Another idea that is central to deflationism is that *truth does not define a genuine predicate.* It is not, however, entirely clear what this means.

> "M. Williams indicates that the burden is on those who oppose the deflationary thesis to give us a reason why we should think that 'is true' is a genuine predicate [...] This is a view that cannot be taken seriously [for] it presupposes as the relevant dialectical principle that we should assume that a predicate is not genuine until given a reason to think it is. And that principle in turn implies, given the present undeveloped state of semantics, that it is rational for us to believe the contradiction that *most* predicates are not genuine predicates." [18], page 331.

Since by definition most predicates *are* genuine predicates, Kirkham thereby places on the deflationist the burden of showing otherwise in the case of truth. As an example of this, Simon Blackburn argues that a genuine predicate extends to a unified class of objects that share common features. The predicate 'is true' is not like this.

> "We know *individually* what makes this predicate applicable to the judgements or sentences of an understood language. 'Penguins waddle' is a true sentence, in English, if and only if penguins waddle. It is true that snow is white if and only if snow is white. The reason the first sentence deserves the predicate is that penguins waddle, and the reason why the judgement that snow is white deserves the predicate is that snow *is* white. But these reasons are entirely different. There is no single account, or even little family of accounts, in virtue of which each deserves the predicate." [2], page 230.

Since there are as many different reasons why a sentence deserves the predicate as there are sentences, there can be no unified account of why any given sentence should be called true.

But even if truth is not a property in the sense that Blackburn requires, perhaps it is still a property of some sort. Paul Horwich believes that,

> "'is true' is a perfectly good English predicate.

What the minimalist wishes to emphasise, however, is that truth is not a complex or naturalistic property but a property of some other kind." [15]

This brings us to Willard Quine's view that the truth predicate is merely a logical device for *disquotation* [24]. Presented with a sentence, we can obtain the conditions under which it is true by disquoting and removing the reference to truth. For example, if we want to know under what conditions *'snow is white' is true*, we remove the quotation marks and truth predicate, to leave the necessary and sufficient condition that *snow is white*. It follows that,

"Truth is a property all right; but it is just that property whose expression in a language gives that language a device for cancelling semantic ascent. There is no more to the property than that." [6] page 137.

It has been objected that because the preceding theories take *sentences* to be the truth bearers, "deflationism makes the notion of truth language-relative" whereas "the notion of truth does

30

not seem to be language relative at all." [27] Of course, this criticism also applies to substantive theories where sentences are the truth bearers. However, there are deflationary theories that take propositions as the truth bearers.

Horwich proposed the *minimalist* theory of truth. This bears some similarity to Ramsey's theory. Horwich is doubtful of *synonymy* between p and *it is true that p*, but endorses a weaker *material equivalence*. Thus we have the following *T-sentences*, one for each proposition p:

the proposition that p is true iff p

The minimalist expresses his version of deflationism by stating that the collection of all such T-sentences expresses all that there is to be said about truth:

"In order for the truth predicate to fulfil its function we must acknowledge that

(MT)   The proposition that *quarks really exist* is true if and only if quarks really exist, the proposition that *lying is bad* is true if and only if lying is bad, ... and so on; *but nothing more about truth need be assumed.* The entire conceptual and theoretical role of truth may be explained on this basis." [15]

Although Horwich calls his minimalist theory a 'deflationary attitude toward truth', he remains neutral on the issue of whether truth is a genuine property, declaring

> "Minimalism does not involve, in itself, any particular answer to this question. For it may be combined with a variety of different conceptions of property, some of which will yield the conclusion that the truth predicate does stand for a property, and some that it doesn't." [15]

There is, however, serious doubt as to whether Horwich really does provide a definition for the truth of propositions. Donald Davidson notes a difficulty of interpreting the T-sentences of Horwich's schema:

> "the same sentence appears twice in instances of Horwich's schema, once after the words 'the proposition that', in a context that requires the result to be a singular term, the subject of a predicate, and once *as an ordinary sentence*. We

cannot eliminate this iteration of the same sentence without destroying all appearance of a theory. But we cannot understand the result of the iteration unless we can see how to make use of the same semantic features of the repeated sentence in both of its appearances." [5], page 318 (italics mine).

Of course, the problem can be resolved by modifying the T-sentences to read

the proposition expressed by the *sentence p* is true iff *p*

but this, once again, makes truth a language relative notion. Furthermore, Kirkham has noted that defining truth for languages that we do not understand is problematic for minimalism:

"I can give no sense to 'is (minimally) true' when predicated of a sentence that I do not understand or when predicated of a thought state of a person whose language I do not understand. [...] Horwich would admit that minimal truth is not defined for languages we do not understand in the sense that we cannot express the clauses of MT for sentences (thought states) in such languages." [18], page 342.

In view of these difficulties, it is not clear that Horwich's theory improves upon that of Quine.

1.4 The Paradox of the Liar Introduced

Having reviewed the debate between substantive and deflationary accounts of truth, we turn to a central obstacle for theories in both camps, namely the semantic paradoxes. Just as the discovery of set theoretical paradoxes had considerable impact upon the development of set theory, semantic paradoxes have influenced the development of semantics. Perhaps the most important of these, the paradox of the liar, is believed to have originated from Epimenides of Crete, who is said to have proclaimed "All Cretans are liars!" Although Epimenides' proclamation is not strictly paradoxical (for example, even a liar need not speak falsely *always*) modern formulations of the paradox are not so easily dissolved. The usual way of formulating the paradox is by forming a sentence which asserts its own falsity, thus:

This sentence is false

If the pronoun 'this' is objected to, then the same effect may be achieved more subtly by a device such as:

The sentence in bold type on page 35 of ISBN 978-0-9935945-4-0 is false

In whatever way it is achieved the outcome is the same: we have a sentence that if assumed to be true then, by virtue of its content, must be false and if assumed to be false then must be true. Merely banning such a sentence does not help. We often wish to construct a sentence that asserts the truth or falsity of *another* sentence. But if this is permitted, then we can construct a pair of paradoxical sentences thus:

(S_1) S_2 is true

(S_2) S_1 is false

Indeed we shall see that for a collection of sentences

some of which declare others to be true or false, there is nothing in the intrinsic structure of the sentences that determines whether or not paradox arises. In certain circumstances this can depend upon contingent facts. At any rate, immunity from paradox cannot be guaranteed merely by banning certain troublesome sentences from our language. The consequences of the liar paradox are extremely serious, since we are forced to conclude that our ordinary understanding of truth expressed in the equivalence schema is inconsistent.

A number of approaches to resolving the paradox have been attempted, and I describe here a few of the more important ones. Since a contradiction ensues when either of the values 'true' or 'false' is assigned to the liar sentence, we might wonder whether the paradox might be resolved by allowing the liar sentence to take *both* truth values, or indeed *neither* truth value.

In the truth glut approach the paradox is benignly tolerated, and the liar sentence is allowed to be *both* true and false. Whilst this might resolve the problem, it creates considerable further difficulties. If a theory has a sentence p that is both true and false, then we can prove *any* sentence whatsoever. Let q be any sentence. Consider the conditional $p \rightarrow q$. Since p is false, the conditional statement is true. But since p is also true, we have both p and $p \rightarrow q$ and so by modus ponens we can infer that q is true.

Clearly a formal system in which we can prove *anything whatsoever* is going to be less than satisfactory. Attempts have been made to salvage something from this situation by disallowing the use of the modus ponens inference rule. This creates another difficulty, for although it prevents the indiscriminate proof of all sentences, it also disallows the use of modus ponens in non-paradoxical situations, effectively crippling logic. It is possible to construct logics in which modus ponens is *selectively* allowed in the unproblematic situations. However, this seems artificial and somewhat ad hoc.

At the opposite extreme, attempts have been made to resolve the paradox by relaxing the principle of bivalence and allowing that certain sentences be neither true nor false, for example by introducing a third truth value. There are different ways of doing this, according to what the third value is supposed to signify. A discussion of many-valued logics may be found in [14] Chapter 11.

The third truth value may signify that a sentence is *indeterminate*; it is neither true nor false, being *unsettled* in its truth value. With this intuition in mind, we may specify truth values for compound sentences. Where a sentence is indeterminate, its negation is also indeterminate. Disjunctions and conjunctions of sentences are dealt with according to the following tables:

∨	F	T	I
F	F	T	I
T	T	T	T
I	I	T	I

∧	F	T	I
F	F	F	F
T	F	T	I
I	F	I	I

This is the strong three-valued logic of Kleene. We can neutralise the liar sentence by allowing it to be *indeterminate*. Since the liar sentence and its negation are both indeterminate, no contradiction arises.

Unfortunately, this approach falls to a slightly different paradox known as the *strengthened liar*. This may be formulated as:

> this sentence is not true

or more explicitly as:

> this sentence is either false or indeterminate

Supposing this to be true, then it is either false or indeterminate; supposing it to be false, then it is true; supposing it to be indeterminate, it is true. In each case, a contradiction arises.

Alternatively, the third value may signify that a sentence is *meaningless*. The negation of a meaningless sentence is meaningless, and any conjunction or disjunction involving a meaningless sentence is also meaningless. Hence we arrive at somewhat different tables from those above. However, a formulation of the strengthened liar as:

> this sentence is either false or meaningless

will still be paradoxical under this scheme. Furthermore, allowing still more truth values is to no avail; strengthened liar sentences may be formulated that are tailored to defeat every attempt. In view of this, it is not surprising that this version of the paradox is sometimes known as the *persistent* liar.

A subtly different approach was proposed by Kripke. Rather than introducing a third truth value, he devised a theory under which certain sentences *lack* truth value. I discuss Kripke's suggestion in Chapter 5.

1.5 The Language Levels Approach

Any natural language is able to make assertions about its own expressions. For example we may say, in English, that the noun 'snow' in English *refers* to snow, or that the property 'is wet' in English is *satisfied* by water. In a similar way, we can state, in English, that a given sentence of English is *true*. We call languages with this property *semantically closed*. Tarski held that it is precisely this that leads to the semantic paradoxes.

This led Tarski to develop his language levels approach to the problem of defining *true sentence* for formalised languages. The idea is that one needs to distinguish the language that one is trying to develop semantics *for* from the language *in which* the semantics are developed. Tarski was perhaps the first to recognise that these need not be the same language.

An analogy may be helpful. Suppose that a group of English speakers are learning German. In this context German is the *object language*. The class might be conducted using English, augmented by *quoted* expressions from German. In this context the augmented English is the *metalanguage*. The metalanguage has two essential features:

- the ability to *quote* from the object language;

- the ability to *translate* expressions of the object language.

The English is used to 'point to' words and phrases in German and explain what they mean in English. For example, the meaning of the object language sentence

Kohle ist schwartz

is given by the metalanguage sentence

"Kohle ist schwartz" means that coal is black.

Suppose now that we have a fragment of English L containing some names and predicates but, importantly, *not* a truth predicate. In order to provide a definition of truth in L we need to construct a metalanguage L^+, with a truth predicate whose domain is the set of sentences of L. As with our example about English speakers learning German, the metalanguage must be able to quote from L, and to provide a translation of each expression of L. This second requirement is readily satisfied by allowing L^+ to contain L as a subset, so that the translation of each object language sentence S into L^+ is S itself.

Consider the following sentence of L:

snow is white

We assert the truth of this sentence by means of the appropriate sentence of L^+:

"snow is white" is true

We may now construct our first partial definition of truth using the language levels approach. When is the sentence "snow is white" true? Surely in just those cases where snow is white. So we make the following definition:

> "snow is white" is true iff snow is white

This only defines truth for one sentence of L. The definition can be expanded for any finite number of sentences thus:

> S is true iff (S is "snow is white" and snow is white) or (S is "coal is black" and coal is black) or ...

with one clause for each sentence of L. Part of Tarski's technical achievement was to show how such a definition could be given recursively for languages with an infinite number of sentences.

We now examine what happens when we attempt to construct the liar paradox. Consider

> (λ) λ is not true

Because λ contains the truth predicate applicable to sentences of L, it is a sentence of the metalanguage L^+, but *not* a sentence of L. Since it is not a sentence of L, it follows trivially that λ is not a *true* sentence of L, and no paradox arises. (Jeffrey Ketland has observed that since "λ is not true-in-L" is materially equivalent to λ, by the definition of the strengthened liar, we have thereby *derived* the strengthened liar sentence in the metalanguage L^+! [17])

To complete our description of the language levels approach, suppose that we now wish to define truth for sentences of L^+, for example

""snow is white" is true" is true

To do so, we would need to ascend to a meta-metalanguage L^{++} containing a new truth predicate whose domain is the set of sentences of L^+. Continuing in this way, an infinite hierarchy of languages may be constructed, each containing its own truth predicate whose domain is the set of sentences of the language immediately below it in the hierarchy.

In chapter 2 we introduce *formalised languages*, and in Chapter 3 we describe how Tarski formulated his definition of *true sentence* for such languages.

2
FORMALISED LANGUAGES AND GÖDEL'S THEOREMS

2.1 Formalised Languages and Predicate Calculus

In a natural language the truth of a given sentence can depend upon a variety of non-linguistic factors, such as who is asserting the sentence, and when and where it is being asserted. By contrast, in a formalised language the truth of a given sentence depends only upon the *form* of the sentence, that is to say the symbols present and their arrangement, and upon the *interpretation* or meaning of the sentence. We say more about interpretations shortly.

As with the words of a natural language, the symbols

of a formalised language need to be arranged in a particular order to form a sentence. The rules governing the arrangement of symbols are called the *syntax* of the language. The syntax of a formalised language is always carefully specified.

We shall describe the syntax of first order *predicate calculus*. The language *L* has individual *names a, b, c, ...* denoting particular objects (things, people, places, etc.) and *variables x, y, z, ...* thought of as 'gaps' where names may be substituted. *L* also has *predicate letters F, G, H, ...* which stand in place of properties, relations etc.

The simplest type of sentence in the language, an *atomic sentence*, is formed by juxtaposing a predicate with an appropriate number of names. So if *F* is a one-place predicate standing for the property of redness, then '*Fa*' is the sentence that expresses '*a* is red'. We may say that *a satisfies F*. The notion of *satisfaction* will be important in what follows. Similarly, if *G* is a two-place predicate standing for the relation of being taller than, then '*Gbc*' is the sentence that expresses '*b* is taller than *c*'. We may say that the ordered pair (b, c) *satisfies* G.

In a similar way an *atomic open sentence* can be formed by juxtaposing a predicate letter with an appropriate number of variables. Thus the following are atomic open sentences:

$$Fx \qquad Gyz$$

Note that despite the terminology, an open sentence is not strictly speaking a sentence, but becomes one when names are substituted for the variables.

Having specified the syntax of atomic sentences in L, we may use the usual logical operators and connectives to form compound sentences. If ϕ and ψ are sentences of L, then so are the following:

$$(\neg\phi) \qquad (\text{``not } \phi\text{''})$$

$$(\phi \wedge \psi) \qquad (\text{``}\phi \text{ and } \psi\text{''})$$

$$(\phi \vee \psi) \qquad (\text{``}\phi \text{ or } \psi\text{''})$$

$$(\phi \rightarrow \psi) \qquad (\text{``if } \phi \text{ then } \psi\text{''})$$

$$(\phi \leftrightarrow \psi) \qquad (\text{``}\phi \text{ iff } \psi\text{''})$$

Similarly, if ϕ and ψ are open sentences then each of the five compound expressions above is also an open sentence. Notice that we can iterate the rules of sentence formation to produce arbitrarily complex sentences.

An open sentence can be completed to form a sentence either by substituting a name in place of each variable, or by *binding* each variable by using a *quantifier*. A *universal quantifier*, written $(\forall x)$, signifies that the open sentence that follows is satisfied by substituting *any* name in place of x. An *existential quantifier*, written $(\exists x)$, signifies that the open sentence that follows is satisfied by substituting *some* name in place of x.

We turn now to the meaning or semantics of the language, which is supplied by specifying an *interpretation*. An interpretation I of L has a set of objects called the *domain*, written *dom(I)*, over which the variables of L range. I assigns to each name of L a member of *dom(I)*. We may think of this as a mapping from the names of L to *dom(I)* that fixes the *reference* of each name.

I assigns to each one-place predicate letter F of L the *extension* of F, that is the subset of *dom(I)* comprising precisely those members that satisfy F. Similarly I assigns to each two-place predicate letter G of L the subset of $dom(I) \times dom(I)$ comprising precisely those ordered pairs that satisfy G. Similar assignments apply for three or more place predicates. A detailed exposition of interpretations may be found in [4].

Example

Suppose that L has names a, b, c and a one-place predicate letter F.

Let the domain of the interpretation be

$$dom(I) = \{snow, milk, coal\}.$$

For the names, let

$I(a) = snow,\ I(b) = milk,\ I(c) = coal.$ For the predicate let

$$I(F) = \{snow, milk\}.$$

Then the sentences 'Fa' and 'Fb' will be true under the interpretation I. We write

$$I \models Fa \text{ and } I \models Fb$$

and say that I is a *model* for 'Fa' and for 'Fb'. The

sentence '*Fc*' will *not* be true under *I*, so that *I* is *not* a model for '*Fc*'.

We complete this section by introducing the concepts of proof and theory. In a formalised language *L*, a *proof* of a sentence ϕ is a finite sequence of sentences

$$\phi_1, \phi_2, \phi_3, ..., \phi_n$$

such that each ϕ_i is either an axiom, or else follows from two sentences earlier in the sequence by a rule of inference such as *modus ponens*, and such that the final sentence ϕ_n is ϕ. A set *T* of sentences of *L* is called a *theory* if it is closed under deductive consequence. That is, if a sentence ϕ may be proved from members of *T*, then ϕ is itself a member of *T*. The members of *T* are called its *theorems*. If the sentence ϕ is a theorem of *T* we shall write

$$T \vdash \phi.$$

An example that will be of particular importance is the arithmetic of natural numbers. This may be formalised in predicate calculus using the axioms of first order Peano arithmetic, referred to here as *PA* (see Appendix, and see [12] for historical background). Theorems include arithmetic identities, for example

$$PA \vdash 2 \times 2 = 4$$

and algebraic identities, for example

$$PA \vdash (\forall x)(\forall y)(x + y = y + x).$$

Note that by the soundness and completeness theorems for first-order predicate calculus, for any theory T we have

$$T \vdash \phi \quad \text{iff} \quad (\text{if } I \models T \text{ then } I \models \phi)$$

so that theoremhood and model-theoretic satisfaction precisely coincide.

2.2 Gödel's Incompleteness Theorems

Some of the most significant developments in mathematics during the twentieth century concerned the foundations of the subject. An early pioneer in this area was Gottlob Frege, who sought to demonstrate that the propositions of arithmetic of natural numbers could be derived from purely logical laws. Since a significant part of mathematics may be constructed from natural numbers, Frege would thereby show that the truth of mathematics rested upon logic rather than, as believed by J. S. Mill, upon contingent facts. Unfortunately, he was not fully aware that paradoxes somewhat similar to that of the liar could arise within mathematics, in particular in the theory of sets. He was made painfully aware of this when Bertrand Russell wrote to him about such paradoxes in 1902. In an appendix to his Basis Laws Frege writes,

> "Hardly anything more unwelcome can befall a scientific writer than one of the foundations of his edifice be shaken after the work is finished. I have been placed in this position by a letter of Mr. Bertrand Russell just as the printing of this volume was nearing completion." [11]

It is deeply unfortunate, however, that Frege regarded much of his life's work as a failure, because much that he accomplished has contributed greatly to our understanding of the foundations of mathematics and logic, and to the philosophy of language.

In their *Principia Mathematica*, Russell and his

collaborator Alfred Whitehead attempted to derive a large portion of known mathematics from the theory of sets. In his *theory of types* Russell had side-stepped the paradoxes of set theory by distinguishing sets of individuals, sets of sets, sets of sets of sets, and so on. In *Principia Mathematica* he and Whitehead sought to use the theory of types to provide a foundation for mathematics that was both consistent and *complete*, in the sense that all true propositions could be proved. Kurt Gödel's incompleteness theorems showed that what Russell and Whitehead were attempting to do could never be achieved.

I begin with an informal demonstration of incompleteness in English. In a similar manner to the liar sentence that asserts its own falsity, we may construct a sentence that asserts its own *unprovability*:

(G) the sentence G is not provable.

Supposing that G were false, then G not being provable is false; hence G is provable. But if G is provable, then it must be true. Hence the supposition that G is false produces a contradiction. It follows that G must be true, and consequently not provable.

Gödel showed in [13] that the formalised language of *Principia Mathematica* contains a sentence analogous to *G*. It follows that Russell and Whitehead's formal system must be *incomplete*, in that it contains true propositions which cannot be proven within the system. Gödel showed that the problem was not particular to Russell and Whitehead's approach. In *any* theory that is consistent and powerful enough to allow the development of arithmetic of natural numbers, a sentence analogous to *G* can be constructed. Hence any such system is incomplete.

In order to demonstrate the incompleteness of arithmetic Gödel needed to express provability *within the theory PA itself.* The precise details are not important, but he achieved this by assigning a natural number $\lceil \phi \rceil$ to each sentence ϕ. It is then possible to define a proof predicate $prov(\lceil \phi \rceil)$, which 'expresses the provability' of ϕ in *PA*, satisfying

$$(*) \quad PA \vdash \phi \quad \text{iff} \quad PA \vdash prov(\lceil \phi \rceil).$$

This may be used in conjunction with the following important result:

Diagonal Lemma   For any predicate F there is a sentence ϕ of the language such that

$$PA \vdash \phi \leftrightarrow F(\ulcorner \phi \urcorner).$$

By applying the lemma in the case of the negation of the provability predicate, we deduce that there is a sentence G such that

$$PA \vdash G \leftrightarrow \neg prov(\ulcorner G \urcorner),$$

which in effect 'asserts its own unprovability.' This together with (*) leads directly to first of the two incompleteness theorems.

We require PA to be consistent, for otherwise it would be possible to prove *any* sentence, as we remarked in 1.4. We might express this consistency by stating that PA is unable to prove a blatantly false sentence such as '0 = 1', and define

$$Con(PA) = \neg prov(\ulcorner 0 = 1 \urcorner).$$

We may now paraphrase Gödel's theorems as follows:

First Incompleteness Theorem   If PA is consistent then there is a sentence G such that we do not have $PA \vdash G$ or $PA \vdash \neg G$.

Second Incompleteness Theorem If PA is consistent then we do not have $PA \vdash Con(PA)$.

The theorems are actually more general than this, in that any theory that is a consistent extension of Robinson Arithmetic Q (see Appendix) will suffer similar incompleteness.

As we shall see, Tarski claimed that he could provide positive truth theoretic results to match Gödel's negative results, so that given a sufficiently rich theory of truth it becomes possible to fill in the gaps that have been highlighted by the incompleteness theorems.

3
TARSKI'S SEMANTIC CONCEPTION OF TRUTH

3.1 The Aims of Tarski's Theory

Whereas the *syntax* of a language is concerned with the correct arrangement of its symbols to yield well-formed sentences, the *semantics* of a language is concerned with the *meaning* of its expressions. Tarski characterises semantics as

> "a discipline which, speaking loosely, deals with certain relations between expressions of a language and the objects (or 'states of affairs') 'referred to' by those expressions." [31]

Among semantic concepts he reckons *reference* (or denotation) of names, *satisfaction* of predicates, and of course *truth*. Tarski wished to establish semantics as an exact science. The prevailing doctrine of *physicalism* at that time held that in order for a discipline to be scientific it must be reducible to physical, and possibly logical or mathematical, notions. Thus one of the goals of Tarski's work was to define truth is terms of such notions. In practice, as we shall see, he did this by first reducing truth to the semantic notion of satisfaction, and then reducing satisfaction to notions that are physical or logico-mathematical.

Tarski stated that his aim was to give a materially adequate and formally correct definition of the term *true sentence*. His material adequacy requirement is that the theory must entail all instances of the schema:

$$X \text{ is true iff } p$$

where X stands in place of a metalanguage *name* for a sentence of the object language, and p stands for a *translation* of that sentence into the metalanguage. This schema is often called *Convention T*, and its individual instances are often called *T-sentences*. Tarski emphasises that Convention T is *not* itself a definition of truth, but that "the general definition has to be, in a certain sense, a logical conjunction of all these partial definitions." [29]

Tarski's definition may be described more clearly by allowing the metalanguage to contain the object language as a subset and to *quote* from the object language using the quotation operator < >. The *name* X of a sentence will then be the quotation of the sentence, and the *translation* p is replaced by the sentence itself, so that we can express the material adequacy condition as:

$$< \phi > \text{ is true iff } \phi$$

for each sentence ϕ of the object language. Nothing of substance is lost by making this amendment, which Tarski himself employs in [32]. Our metalanguage for illustrative purposes will be English augmented by predicate calculus.

3.2 A Recursive Definition of Truth for a Language Without Quantifiers

To appreciate the technical difficulties that Tarski overcame in giving a definition of truth for formalised languages with quantifiers, it is helpful to first construct a similar definition for a language without quantifiers.

Consider a language L with just a single one-place predicate F and a pair of names a and b. We can form just two atomic sentences, 'Fa' and 'Fb'. We define truth for these as follows:

S is true iff (S is 'Fa' and Fa) or (S is 'Fb' and Fb).

This definition may be extended to a language having any finite number of names and predicate letters, by providing an extra clause for each atomic sentence. Now suppose that we enrich L by allowing the formation of compound sentences using the usual logical operators and connectives. We may form infinitely many sentences, and so the method of definition having a clause for each sentence will no longer serve. However, we may provide a recursive definition for the truth of any sentence as follows:

> S is true iff   (S is '*Fa*' and *Fa*) or
>
> (S is '*Fb*' and *Fb*) or
>
> (S is ($\neg S_1$) and S_1 is not true) or
>
> (S is ($S_1 \lor S_2$) and at least one of
>
> S_1 and S_2 is true).

The connectives $\land$, $\rightarrow$, and $\leftrightarrow$ are taken as defined in terms of $\neg$ and $\lor$ in the usual ways:

$p \land q = \neg(\neg p \lor \neg q)$

$p \rightarrow q = \neg p \lor q$

$p \leftrightarrow q = (p \rightarrow q) \land (q \rightarrow p)$

Example: '$\neg(Fa \lor \neg Fb)$' is true

> iff '$Fa \lor \neg Fb$' is not true
>
> iff it is not the case that at least one of '*Fa*' and '$\neg Fb$' is true
>
> iff it is not the case that, either '*Fa*' is true or '*Fb* ' is not true
>
> iff it is not the case that, either *Fa*, or not *Fb*.

3.3 An Impasse for Languages with Quantifiers and Tarski's Solution

Suppose that we enrich the simple language of the last section with the universal and existential quantifiers. We can now form the following sentences:

$$(\forall x)Fx \qquad\qquad (\exists x)Fx$$

This appears to present no problem. We may treat these as additional atomic sentences and add two clauses to our definition of truth as follows:

> S is true iff   (S is 'Fa' and Fa) or
> (S is 'Fb' and Fb) or
> (S is '$(\forall x)Fx$' and Fx for all x) or
> (S is '$(\exists x)Fx$' and Fx for some x).

Now suppose that we further enrich L by adding a predicate letter G, giving four more atomic sentences:

$$Ga \qquad Gb \qquad (\forall x)Gx \qquad\qquad (\exists x)Gx$$

These may be accommodated by providing the four appropriate clauses of the definition. Compound sentences may be formed that involve quantified statements, for example

$$(\forall x)Fx \lor (\exists x)Gx.$$

These too do not present a problem, as the recursive clauses of the definition will cater for these by iteratively decomposing them into their constituent atomic sentences. The difficulty is that logical connectives can occur *inside the scope of a quantifier* as well as between atomic sentences. Consider the following:

$$(\forall x)(Fx \lor Gx)$$

Because the scope of the universal quantifier includes a disjunction, this sentence cannot be decomposed into atomic sentences.

To surmount this difficulty, Tarski needed to identify some semantic property that could be possessed by open sentences as well as genuine sentences, and then to define truth in terms of that property. The property in question is *satisfaction*.

Tarski's ingenious idea was to carry out the recursive parts of the definition at the level of *satisfaction*, and only then to define truth in terms of satisfaction. We now describe how this is accomplished.

Tarski needed to define satisfaction for open sentences containing an arbitrary number of variables $x_1, x_2, x_3, \ldots$ To achieve this, he stated his definition in terms of satisfaction of sentences by *sequences* of objects. A *sequence* σ of objects is a countably infinite collection of objects arranged in some particular order thus:

$$\sigma_1, \sigma_2, \sigma_3, \ldots$$

Repetition of a given object within a sequence is allowed. The order in which the objects occur is important; if two sequences contain the same objects but have these arranged in a different order then they are distinct sequences.

We explain first how we define satisfaction of a one-place predicate by a sequence:

$$\sigma \text{ satisfies } {}^{'}Fx_i^{'} \text{ iff } F\sigma_i$$

In a similar fashion, for a two-place predicate:

$$\sigma \text{ satisfies } {}^{'}Gx_ix_j^{'} \text{ iff } G\sigma_i\sigma_j$$

Similar definitions may be made for three and higher place predicates. We require one such clause for each predicate letter in the language.

Having defined satisfaction by sequences for the atomic open sentences, we now provide recursive clauses as before in order to cater for the compound open sentences:

σ satisfies $\neg S$ iff σ does not satisfy S

σ satisfies $S_1 \vee S_2$ iff σ satisfies at least one of
$$S_1 \text{ and } S_2$$

Finally, we add clauses to cater for the quantifiers as follows:

σ satisfies $(\forall x_i)S$ iff *any* sequence that differs from σ in at most the i^{th}place satisfies S.

σ satisfies $(\exists x_i)S$ iff *some* squence that differs from σ in at most the i^{th}place satisfies S.

For ease of reference we recount the entire definition:

Tarski's Definition of True Sentence:

σ *satisfies* S iff ($S = Fx_i$ and $F\sigma_i$) or

($S = Gx_ix_j$ and $G\sigma_i\sigma_j$) or

(clause for each predicate) or

($S = \neg S_1$ and σ does not satisfy S_1)   or

($S = S_1 \lor S_2$ and σ satisfies at least one of

S_1 and S_2) or

($S = (\forall x_i)S_1$ and any sequence that differs from σ in at most the ith place satisfies S_1) or ($S = (\exists x_i)S_1$ and some sequence that differs from σ in at most the ith place satisfies S_1).

With these clauses in place, Tarski defines truth in terms of satisfaction by sequences:

S is *true* iff S is satisfied by all sequences σ.

3.4 What Kind of Theory of Truth is Tarski's Theory?

A peculiarity of Tarski's theory is the wide divergence of the ways in which it has been construed. Some advocates of correspondence have seen it as a correspondence theory, whilst deflationists have embraced it as a deflationary theory. Ketland, as we shall see in Chapter 4, wishes to use Tarski's theory to argue against deflationism. Still others have seen in Tarski's work the conclusive proof that truth cannot be defined.

We begin by assessing what Tarski would claim for his own theory. There is superficial textual evidence that Tarski believes that he is providing a modern version of the correspondence theory. He expresses the wish to "catch hold of the actual meaning of an old notion" [31], specifically that expressed by Aristotle in his *Metaphysics*:

"To say of what is that it is not, or of what is not that it is, is false, while to say of what is that it is, or of what is not that it is not, is true."

This, he believes, may be expressed in modern terminology by the following formulae:

> "The truth of a sentence consists in its agreement with (or correspondence to) reality."

> "A sentence is true if it designates an existing state of affairs" both [31]

> "A true sentence is one which says that the state of affairs is so and so, and the state of affairs indeed is so and so." [29]

Whilst these quotes taken in isolation suggest that Tarski really is offering a correspondence theory, upon deeper analysis this seems unlikely. Recall that a correspondence theory is supposed to instantiate the schema

S is true iff S corresponds to X and X obtains

where X is a truthmaker. In particular, such a theory must elucidate the nature of the relation of *correspondence*, and the nature of the truthmakers. Tarski does neither of these things. Furthermore, he tells us that in his construction

> "I will not make use of any semantical concept if I am not able previously to reduce it to other concepts." [29]

On Tarski's understanding of *semantical*, the relation of *correspondence* would be such a concept. Nowhere does he make clear either what this relation is or how it is to be reduced to other concepts of a non-semantical nature. Nor does Tarski give any indication as to the nature of the truthmakers. Whilst this does not imply that his theory is non-substantive, the difficulty in supporting Tarski's claim of providing a modernised version of correspondence has caused many to view it as deflationary. For example, Blackburn:

> "Let us call the connection of truth, reference, and satisfaction the 'neutral core' of Tarski's work. The neutral core connects together truth, reference, and satisfaction. But it gives us no theory of how to break in to this circle; that is, of how to describe what it is about a population which makes it true that any of their words or sentences deserve such semantic descriptions." [2], page 270.

"It is not now very controversial that the neutral core of Tarski's work leaves us with reference, satisfaction and truth in a tight little circle, nor that it would be acceptable to philosophers of any bent: realist, anti-realist, correspondence, coherence, dismissive neutralist or whatever." [2], page 273.

This is unfair to Tarski, since it gives the impression that he has defined each of reference, satisfaction, and truth in terms of the other two. His theory does not make use of the notion of reference, since the language for which he defines truth does not contain any names. Furthermore, truth is to be defined in terms of satisfaction, but not the reverse

For a simple sentence involving just one variable, after stripping away the mention of sequences, the definition would look like this:

$(\exists x)Fx$ is true if and only if there is at least one value of x that satisfies F.

Now whilst it is fair to say that whether or not there is such an x satisfying F is going to be a matter of whether or not is stipulated as having a non-empty extension for the interpretation of the language, there is nothing circular about the definition. Whether or not, for example, there exists an x such that x *is white* will depend upon how the extension of *white* has been specified. However, it might be argued that the role of a theory of *truth* is to guide us as to whether or not particular sentences are *true*; it should not be expected to guide us to whether or not there exist white things.

Tarski's claims for his conception of truth are usually modest. He does not even claim his semantic conception of truth is 'the right one', declaring that

> "I do not understand what is at stake in such disputes; for the problem itself is so vague that no definite solution is possible. In fact, it seems to me that the sense in which the phrase 'the right conception' is used has never been made clear." [31]

He is scathing of the so-called problem of truth, sarcastically remarking

> "I have heard it remarked that the formal definition of truth has nothing to do with 'the philosophical problem of truth.' However,

nobody has ever pointed out to me in an intelligible way just what that problem is." [31]

The tone here suggests that perhaps Tarski does not acknowledge that there *is* such a problem, a view that would be very much in the spirit of deflationism. Hartry Field reminds us that

> "There is of course a strong suggestion of the deflationist viewpoint in Tarski himself, stemming from his famous adequacy condition on truth definitions." [9] page 375

However, Field also argues that there is an important sense in which Tarski's theory is not *fully* deflationary:

> "Even if a Tarskian were to give up the insistence on *defining* truth, there would still be an important difference between the Tarskian approach and the full-fledged deflationary approach [...] Central to what is usually thought of as the Tarskian approach is that truth is characterised (inductively if not explicitly) in terms of compositional structure. This gives compositional principles of truth a much more central role than they have on the full-fledged

deflationary account." [9], page 373.

In chapter 4 we examine Jeffrey Ketland's demonstration of another distinction between Tarski's theory and deflationary theories, namely that the former is *deductively* stronger than the latter.

3.5 Objections to Tarski's Theory

Having examined some of the arguments about how to characterise the Tarskian theory, we turn now to some of the objections and criticisms against Tarski's work that have not been included in the previous section.

Many have complained that Tarski's definition only works relative to the language at hand. That is, rather than defining *truth* he defines *truth-in-L* for a given language *L*. As we saw in 1.3, this same charge has been brought against certain deflationary theories. Indeed, this will be a feature of any theory of truth, deflationary or substantive, that takes the sentences of a language to be the truth bearers. The only way to avoid relativising truth to a language is to take some non-linguistic entitities such as *beliefs* or *propositions* to be the bearers of truth. Now propositions are notoriously difficult entities to work with, indeed there is not even any general agreement as to what these are. Some regard propositions to be the *contents* of declararive sentences, whilst others regard them as *mental* entities (for example Pitcher), and still others identify them with *facts* (for example Armstrong).

Whilst it is the case that Tarski only shows explicitly how to define truth in one language, that of set theory, he does show that the same method is applicable to a broad range of formalised languages. So although two formalised languages will have distinct definitions for the truth predicate, there will be a structural similarity in how the predicate is defined for the two languages.

A related objection, given by Kirkham, is that it would not be possible to extend Tarski's definition to cover clauses of a language that one did not understand. He gives as an example a language in which "$\in \Box \Delta$" is true if and only if snow is white, and "$\varnothing \Diamond \vdash$" is true if and only if snow is green, and points out the difficulty that *we* would have in extending this defintion to cover a sentence such as " $\models \therefore \neg$ ". This objection is not wholly justified, as the formalised languages that Tarski is dealing with have a prescribed syntax of predicates and variables. Given a sentence $(\exists x)Fx$ one does not need to know the *meaning* of F in order to give the required clause in the defintion. The sentence is true just in case there is an x that satisfies F. A final objection to Tarski's theory is the difficulty in applying it to natural languages. Tarski himself describes the problem of defining truth for natural languages as meeting with "unsuperable difficulties". Among these difficulties he cites that natural language is not bounded, in the sense that new words can always be added to it, and the difficulty in specifying the structure of expressions that are to count as sentences. Moreover, we have already seen in 1.6 how the semantic closure of natural languages leads to the formulation of semantic paradoxes.

Nevertheless, some hope might be held out that at least *portions* of a natural language, such as those dealing with an empirical science might be sufficiently formalised to allow the application of Tarskian methods. Such portions of a natural language need not be semantically closed, since there is not usually a need to an emprical science to refer to the semantics of its own expressions.

We shall see in Chapter 5 how Saul Kripke constructed a theory of truth using truth gaps which, although not semantically closed, allows a language to contain its own truth predicate. If certain formal difficulties can be overcome for the Kripkean approach, then it may provide a better candidate for the formalisation of natural languages where a truth predicate is required.

4
THE
KETLAND-SHAPIRO
ARGUMENT

4.1 Conservativeness and Deflationism

In this chapter I discuss the results presented in a paper by Jeffrey Ketland [16]. In this work, he argues that Tarski's theory gives a more complete account of truth than a variety of deflationary theories. A similar line of argument was employed by Stewart Shapiro in [28]. These claims rely upon a property of theories called *conservativeness*, to which we now turn.

Suppose that T is a theory expressed in the language of first order predicate calculus. T may be enriched by the addition of further axioms, together with their consequences, to give a theory T^*. We say that T^* is an *extension* of T.

If T^* has only the theorems of T itself, and no more, we say that T^* is a *conservative* extension of T. On the other hand, if T^* has theorems that were not theorems of T then we say that T^* is a *non-conservative* extension of T.

Ketland argues that deflationary theories always produce conservative extensions:

> "*if* truth is non-substantial - as the deflationists claim - *then* the theory of truth *should* be conservative. Roughly: *non-substantiality* ≡ *conservativeness.*"

By contrast, Tarski's theory can in certain circumstances produce a non-conservative extension. It is in precisely this sense that the latter is claimed to be non-deflationary. Shapiro remarks upon how surprising this ought to be for the deflationist:

> "If truth/satisfaction is not substantial - as the deflationist contends - then we should not need to invoke truth in order to establish any results not involving truth explicitly." [28] page 497.

In order to examine Ketland's claims, we must first

clarify exactly what he takes to be a deflationary theory of truth. He examines three such theories. The first of these he characterises by what he calls the *redundancy schema*:

the proposition that p is true if and only if p

He associates such a theory with Ramsey, although as we have seen Ramsey's redundancy theory is actually an attempt to fulfil the speech-act project whereas the above schema is an attempted fulfilment of the metaphysical project. He also compares this theory to the *minimalist theory* of Horwich who, as per the schema, takes *propositions* as truth-bearers. Since Ketland is concerned only with language relative definitions, the comparison is justified only in part. The theories he uses are better characterised by the schema

the sentence $'p'$ is true if and only if p

He uses this to characterise his second deflationary candidate, the *disquotational* theory. Ketland formalises both of these theories in the same way, using the axiom schema

$$Tr(<\phi>) \leftrightarrow \phi,$$

where ϕ is any sentence of L. We shall call the theory obtained from this schema *DT*. In effect, this is to take the totality of T-sentences as a theory of truth. Ketland also considers a *substitutional disquotation* theory, but we omit this here.

4.2 Demonstration that *DT* Produces Conservative Extensions

I shall present Ketland's proof that the extension $T \cup DT$ of any theory T is conservative.

Suppose that T is expressed in the language L, with an interpretation I. We construct the *metalanguage* L^+ with the requisite properties, namely:

- the ability to *quote* from L

- the ability to translate expressions of L into L^+

To fulfil the first of these, L^+ is provided with a *quotation operator* that forms in L^+ a name $<\varepsilon>$ of any expression ε of L. As previously noted, the second requirement can be fulfilled by allowing L^+ to contain the actual expressions of L.

L^+ contains an additional predicate Tr, the truth predicate, that was not present in L. We can form a metalanguage sentence $Tr(<\phi>)$ for each sentence ϕ of L.

The interpretation I may be expanded to an interpretation I^+ of L^+. Since L^+ contains, in addition to the names in L, names for the *sentences* of L, the domain of I^+ is expanded to include these. Letting $sent(L)$ be the set of sentences of L we set

$$dom(I^+) = dom(I) \cup sent(L).$$

The quotation of a sentence of L is to be interpreted as that sentence in the domain, so that

$$I^+(<\phi>) = \phi \text{ for any } \phi \in sent(L).$$

Finally, the truth predicate is interpreted as

$$I^+(Tr) = \{\phi : I \models \phi\},$$

that is the set of all sentences for which I is a model.

Lemma I^+ is a model of DT.

To prove this, we observe that I is a model of some sentence ϕ of L (that is $I \models \phi$) iff ϕ belongs to the extension of the truth predicate in L^+, that is $\phi \in I^+(Tr)$, which is iff I^+ is a model of $Tr(<\phi>)$, that is $I^+ \models Tr(<\phi>)$.

Next, we observe that because I^+ coincides with I on sentences of L, we have

$$I \models \phi \text{ iff } I^+ \models \phi.$$

Combining these observations we obtain

$$I^+ \models Tr(<\phi>) \text{ iff } I^+ \models \phi$$

and hence

$$I^+ \models Tr(<\phi>) \leftrightarrow \phi$$

for each sentence ϕ of L. These are the axioms of DT, so we have

$$I^+ \models DT.$$

∎

Now let T be a theory expressed in L, and let $T \cup DT$ be the extended theory obtained from T by adding the axioms of DT. Then we have:

$T \cup DT$ is a conservative extension of T

Suppose that there is a sentence ϕ of L which is a theorem of $T \cup DT$, but which is *not* a theorem of T itself, so that

$$T \cup DT \vdash \phi, \text{ but not } T \vdash \phi.$$

Now since ϕ cannot be derived from T, there must be some model for T that is a model for the negation of ϕ, so that

$$I \models \neg\phi.$$

We extend I to give a model I^+ of $T \cup DT$, as before, coinciding with I on sentences of L, so that

$$I^+ \models \neg\phi.$$

But I^+ is a model of $T \cup DT$, that is $I^+ \models T \cup DT$, and $T \cup DT \vdash \phi$ (our hypothesis). It follows that

$$I^+ \models \phi,$$

which in conjunction with the previous statement

yields a contradiction. Hence there can be no theorem of $T \cup DT$ which was not already a theorem of T itself.

■

4.3 Extending Peano Arithmetic Using Tarski's Theory

I now present Ketland's argument that extending a theory by adding the axioms for Tarski's semantic theory, referred to as TS, can produce a non-conservative extension. This is central to the claim that TS provides a more complete account of truth than DT.

The argument makes use of the theory of first order Peano Arithmetic, PA. Recall from 2.2 that Gödel's first incompleteness theorem shows that a sentence G can be formulated in the language of PA such that neither G or its negation are theorems of PA. Recall also that Gödel's second incompleteness theorem shows that the sentence asserting the *consistency* of PA, written $Con(PA)$, is not a theorem of PA.

We extend PA by adding the axioms of Tarski's

theory to produce the extension $PA \cup TS$. Ketland's strategy is to show that although not theorems of PA, both G and $Con(PA)$ are theorems of the extended theory $PA \cup TS$.

As Ketland acknowledges, these facts were already implicit in Tarski's work:

> "All sentences constructed according to Gödel's method possess the property that it can be established whether they are true or false on the basis of the metatheory of higher order having a correct definition of truth." [29]

> "The establishment of scientific semantics, and in particular the definition of truth, enables us to match the negative results in the field of metamathematics with corresponding positive ones, and in that way to fill to some extent the gaps which have been revealed in the deductive method and in very structure of deductive science." [30]

We turn now to the technical details of Ketland's proofs. He requires the following:

Lemma $PA \cup TS \vdash (\forall x)(prov(x) \to Tr(x)).$

Intuitively, this says that any sentence that is provable within *PA* is *true* under the added Tarskian theory. This is a result from Tarski [29]. Tarski's method of proof is, roughly, to demonstrate that each axiom of *PA* is true (in the standard interpretation as the set of natural numbers), and then to show that the rules of inference preserve truth, so that all theorems of *PA* are true. The proof of this lemma relies upon extending the induction schema of *PA* to the truth predicate. This is a key issue in the discussion in 4.5.

Truth Theoretic Result for First

Incompleteness Theorem

The Gödel sentence *G* of *PA* 'asserts its own unprovability', that is

$$PA \vdash G \leftrightarrow \neg prov(\ulcorner G \urcorner) \text{ or equivalently,}$$
$$PA \vdash \neg G \leftrightarrow prov(\ulcorner G \urcorner)$$

Applying the lemma we have

$$PA \cup TS \vdash prov(\ulcorner G \urcorner) \to Tr(\ulcorner G \urcorner)$$

and hence

$$PA \cup TS \vdash \neg G \to Tr(\ulcorner G \urcorner).$$

By the material adequacy of *TS* we have

$$TS \vdash Tr(\ulcorner G \urcorner) \to G.$$

which combined with the previous statement yields

$$PA \cup TS \vdash \neg G \to G$$

The definition of the conditional $\phi \to \psi$ as $\neg\phi \vee \psi$ allows us to conclude

$$PA \cup TS \vdash G$$

as required.

■

Truth Theoretic Result for Second Incompleteness Theorem

From the lemma we have

$$PA \cup TS \vdash prov(\ulcorner 0 = 1 \urcorner) \to Tr(\ulcorner 0 = 1 \urcorner).$$

By the material adequacy of *TS* we have

$$TS \vdash Tr(\ulcorner 0 = 1 \urcorner) \to 0 = 1.$$

From these we obtain

$$PA \cup TS \vdash prov(\ulcorner 0 = 1 \urcorner) \to 0 = 1$$

and by contraposition

$$PA \cup TS \vdash \neg(0 = 1) \to \neg prov(\ulcorner 0 = 1 \urcorner).$$

Now since $PA \vdash \neg(0 = 1)$ we have

$$PA \cup TS \vdash \neg prov(\ulcorner 0 = 1 \urcorner)$$

that is

$$PA \cup TS \vdash Con(PA)$$

as required.

∎

In case any misunderstanding should arise at this point, it is important to appreciate that these results are not *counterexamples* to Gödel's theorems. All that is claimed, is that the Gödel sentence G of PA and the consistency sentence $Con(PA)$ of PA *can* be derived in the enhanced theory $PA \cup TS$, even though these may not be derived in PA itself. Gödel's theorems are still applicable to $PA \cup TS$, so that this too has its own Gödel sentence, G^*, which will not be derivable in $PA \cup TS$. Similarly, the consistency of $PA \cup TS$ is not derivable within *that* theory.

4.4 Ketland and Deflationism

I now discuss Ketland's attempt to expose deflationary theories as incomplete accounts of truth. I begin by noting in passing relevance to the debate in the philosophy of mind as to how, if at all, human intelligence differs from that of machines or computers. Roger Penrose believes that Gödel's theorems show that human intelligence can gain certain insights that cannot be arrived at by mechanistic procedures.

"We shall need to employ *insights* from outside the system - just as we did in order to see that [the Gödel sentence] was a true proposition in the first place. It is these insights that cannot be systematized - and, indeed, must lie outside any algorithmic action." [23] page 143

"A conclusion from the argument concerning Gödel's theorem was that, at least in mathematics, conscious contemplation can sometimes enable one to ascertain the truth of a statement in a way that no algorithm could."

[23] page 532

We have seen in 4.3 that what Penrose supposes to be an insight that can only be arrived at by conscious contemplation, can be derived in an entirely systematic way by enriching PA with a suitable theory of truth. Ketland concludes,

> "Although I am inclined to *disagree* with the computational theory of mind, I think they are wrong on this matter, for G is deducible from the strengthened theory."

Ketland's abstract opens by declaring

> "Deflationism about truth is a pot-pourri, variously claiming that truth is redundant, or is constituted by the totality of 'T-sentences', or is a purely logical device"

and he claims that his results "suggest that Tarskian theories of truth are not redundant or dispensable." We observed in Chapter 1 that there is no unified doctrine of deflationism. Different theories exhibit a variety of features, but usually make one or more of the following claims:

1. truth is *redundant* (Ramsey and the speech-act project) apart from its uses in semantic ascent (Quine and disquotation) for example in making compendious assertions.

2. the truth predicate does not name a *genuine property* (as held for example by Blackburn);

3. the totality of T-sentences gives a complete account of truth (the *minimalism* of Horwich).

We need to clarify which elements of deflationist doctrine Ketland is attempting to refute. The first of these claims, as we have seen, has limited scope. Even advocates of redundancy theories themselves acknowledge *some* uses for a truth predicate, particularly in indirect or compendious assertions. Ketland's argument shows that a truth predicate gives us not only greater powers of expression but, given the correct formulation, greater deductive power too.

With regard to the second claim, we have seen that

Horwich's minimalism is neutral on the issue of whether or not truth is a genuine property. Furthermore, Tarski also seems to be neutral on this. Ketland's work does not alter this position. Hence there is no reason to prefer either *TS* or *DT* with respect to the second claim. In this sense, both are equally deflationary.

However, the third claim, that of minimalism, seems clearly refuted in Ketland's work. He shows that the Tarskian theory enables one to derive results that the minimalist *DT* cannot.

We have already remarked upon Tarski's silence with regard to truthmakers. Neither his work nor Ketland's contradicts those who reject correspondence theories because of their ontological commitment to truthmakers.

Often the motivation for embracing deflationism seems to be flight from the perceived dismal failure of the traditional substantive theories of pragmatism, coherence, and correspondence. Indeed, it seems to be the *negative* features of such substantive theories rather than any positive attraction to the deflationary theories that has resulted in the popularity of the latter. For example, having rejected facts as worldly entities, Dodd says that we are enabled to

> "appreciate the untenability of correspondence theories; and once we achieve this insight, we are left free to adopt a deflationary theory." [6] p.132.

But, is it sufficient motivation to adopt a theory that we be *left free to do so*? Could it be that in our flight from correspondence theories to deflationism, we run too far? The results presented by Ketland suggest that this is the case. Minimalism, we have seen, is simply *too* minimal. It lacks the deductive power of the Tarskian theory. But if we are free to accept deflationism, we are equally free to accept the Tarskian theory. The latter avoids the difficulties encountered by correspondence, but surpasses the minimalist theory by giving a more complete account of truth.

4.5 Three Criticisms

The Ketland-Shapiro argument involves a contentious assumption. This concerns the induction axiom schema of Peano Arithmetic, *PA*:

$$(IND) \quad (F\mathbf{0} \wedge (\forall x)(Fx \to F(x+1))) \to (\forall x)Fx$$

where *F* is any predicate expressible in the language of *PA*. Informally, this says that if **0** satisfies *F* and for each number x satisfying *F* its successor $x+1$ also satisfies *F*, then *all* numbers satisfy *F*. The extended theory $PA \cup TS$ contains an additional predicate, that of truth, *Tr*. The dilemma is, whether or not this axiom schema may be applied to predicates that involve or include *Tr*. The lemma in 4.3 assumes that this has been answered in the affirmative. If this is not the case, then adding Tarski's theory will yield a conservative extension of *PA*. *TS* would then have no greater proof-theoretic strength than *DT*. The extension of *IND* to the truth predicate does seem intuitively reasonable. As Shapiro says

> "Whether one is a deflationist or not, there is no good reason to demur from the extension

of the induction scheme [...] If someone admits that the extension of T is well-defined, then he must admit formulas containing T into the induction scheme." [28] pages 500 and 501.

Others are not convinced that this refutes deflationism in the minimalist sense. In his response to Shapiro, Hartry Field argues that such an extension of *IND* would have consequences incompatible with deflationism only if the instances of *IND* so formed are *essential to truth*. Hence the argument rests on an equivocation with the phrase 'essential to truth', which Field interprets as meaning *depending only upon the nature of truth*. By contrast, regarding instances of *IND* involving *Tr*, he states

"what they depend upon is a fact about the natural numbers, namely, that they are linearly ordered with each element having only finitely many predecessors." [10] page 538.

He concludes

"The commitment to extend induction to newly introduced predicates has nothing special to do with truth: it applies to all predicates, not just truth. So it is hard to see how one's theory of truth could have any special relevance to it."

[10] page 540.

How this dilemma is to be settled is an ongoing debate. I am sceptical about Field's objection, and will sketch my reasons, albeit that I am not sure they are conclusive. We have observed that adding DT to any theory gives a conservative extension. Field wishes to licence a further step, that of adding general laws governing the composition of sentences, such as that for disjunction

$$Tr(\langle p \vee q \rangle) \text{ iff } Tr(\langle p \rangle) \text{ or } Tr(\langle q \rangle)$$

He claims

"It is more interesting to add truth in a way that includes the general laws, since I think it is clear that without such general laws the truth predicate would not serve its main purpose."
[10] page 535

He has in mind here the use of the truth predicate in expressing generalisations that cannot otherwise be readily expressed. Field continues:

> "Let us concede that not only are the Tarski
> biconditionals 'essential to truth', so too are the
> general laws used in so many applications of the
> notion of truth."   [10] page 537.

For example, consider the rule for the truth of a disjunction of sentences. Individual instances of the rule

$$Tr(\langle p \vee q \rangle) \text{ iff } Tr(\langle p \rangle) \text{ or } Tr(\langle q \rangle)$$

for particular sentences p and q may be derived from DT. However the general law

For all p and q, $Tr(\langle p \vee q \rangle)$ iff $Tr(\langle p \rangle)$ or $Tr(\langle q \rangle)$

cannot be derived from DT. Thus, for example, we are unable to derive from DT the general law that 'the disjunction of any sentence and its negation is *true*'.

The situation is somewhat analgous to Robinson arithmetic Q compared with Peano arithmetic PA (see appendix). Robinson arithmetic Q is, roughly speaking, PA without the induction schema. Q is able to prove individual instances of arithmetic laws but not their generalisations. For example, for any pair of natural numbers named by **m** and **n**, we have

$$Q \vdash m + n = n + m$$

But we do *not* have the general law that

$$Q \vdash (\forall x)(\forall y)(x + y = y + x)$$

It should be empahsised that Q is a very comprehensive theory of arithmetic that allows us to deduce many facts about the arithmetic of specific natural numbers, and is even strong enough for Gödel's incompleteness theorems to be applicable. Hence induction is not essential to arithmetic. But without the induction schema crucial general algebraic laws cannot be proved.

I shall argue here that the induction schema is more properly viewed as a logical principle than as a principle of arithmetic. Firstly, recall the rule of *modus ponens:*

From premisses ϕ and $\phi \rightarrow \psi$ we may deduce ψ.

Suppose that the domain consists of a finite number of objects $a_0, a_1, a_2, ..., a_n$. Suppose also that for a predicate F we have Fa_0 and that we also have conditional statements $Fa_{i-1} \rightarrow Fa_i$ for each $i = 1, 2, ..., n$.

From Fa_0 and $Fa_0 \rightarrow Fa_1$ we may deduce Fa_1 by *modus ponens*.

From Fa_1 and $Fa_1 \rightarrow Fa_2$ we may deduce Fa_2 by *modus ponens*.

Continuing in this way, after n applications of *modus ponens* we may deduce Fa_i for all i. Notice that this argument follows from the validity of statements of propositional logic alone, not upon any fact about the natural numbers. In particular, this is valid:

$$Fa_0 \wedge (Fa_0 \rightarrow Fa_1) \wedge (Fa_1 \rightarrow Fa_2) \wedge ... \\ \wedge (Fa_{n-1} \rightarrow Fa_n) \rightarrow Fa_0 \wedge Fa_1 \wedge ... \wedge Fa_n$$

The axiom schema *IND* extends this argument to a linearly ordered countably infinite domain of objects $a_0, a_1, a_2, ...$ Once again, given Fa_0 and conditional statements $Fa_{i-1} \rightarrow Fa_i$ for each $i = 1, 2, ...$ we may deduce Fa_i for all i by continued application of *modus ponens*.

It is this extension of a logical principle from the finite to the countably infinite that gives *PA* the power to deduce general algebraic laws that cannot be deduced from *Q*; similarly, extending *IND* to the truth predicate *Tr* in *TS* allows us to deduce general laws about truth that cannot be deduced from *DT*.

A second criticism of Ketland's paper is that he specifically advocates *Tarski's* theory, rather than any other semantic theory of truth. His results require only two properties of *TS*, namely 'half' of the material adequacy condition:

$$TS \vdash Tr(\ulcorner \phi \urcorner) \rightarrow \phi \text{ for each sentence } \phi$$

and the lemma ensuring that all theorems are *true*:

$$T \cup TS \vdash (\forall x)(prov(x) \rightarrow Tr(x)).$$

It follows that any semantic theory of truth having these two properties will allow the derivation of results that parallel those presented by Ketland for *TS*.

Indeed, it is surprising that Tarski's theory should still be preferred, in view of the developments in set theory to resolve set-theoretical paradoxes. The most fundamental of these is Russell's paradox: let R be the set of all those sets that are *not* elements of themselves. Then R is an element of itself if and only if R is *not* an element of itself, resulting in contradiction. Russell's solution to the problem was his *theory of types*, in which sets of individuals, sets of sets, sets of sets of sets, and so on, are distinguished. The elements of a set of given type must always be of the type immediately below in the hierarchy. This does not allow any set to be a member of itself, and thus resolves the paradox.

The similarity of Russell's theory of types to the Tarski language levels is clear. Tarski's theory is, in effect, a theory of types for sentences. It distinguishes sentences of the object language, the metalanguage, the meta-metalanguage, and so on, with each language level predicating truth only of sentences of the level immediately below in the hierarchy.

However Russell's theory of types has fallen out of favour. In recent decades there has been an overwhelming preference for set theories such of that of Zermelo and Frankel, and that of Von Neummann, Bernays and Gödel. Both of these ensure consistency by disallowing certain collections, such as *R*, from being sets (an introduction to such theories is given in [20]). They are *type free*, in the sense that there is no hierarchy of different types of set.

In view of the success of type-free set theories, it might be expected that type-free semantic theories would be better suited to resolving the semantic paradoxes. Indeed much has been achieved in this area, as Solomon Feferman remarks:

> "On the semantical side there has been an (equally) extensive pursuit of type-free frameworks, especially by workers in philosophical logic. This is partly motivated by the fact that natural language abounds with directly or indirectly self-referential yet apparently harmless expressions - all of which

are excluded from the Tarskian framework. Fretting about the severe restrictions placed by that solution, philosophers have sought to liberalize semantic theory while still blocking the paradoxes." [7]

We consider the type free theory proposed by Saul Kripke in the next chapter.

Finally, another objection is sometimes raised against Tarski's work is, given its technical nature, whether it is relevant to the philosophical issues surrounding truth at all. The sceptic, on enquiring why Tarski's theory is superior to the deflationary *DT*, is told that the former allows the derivation of the Gödel sentence in Peano arithmetic and of the consistency of that arithmetic. Since these matters have little impact upon questions of mainstream philosophy, it is easy to see how they might be dismissed as irrelevant. Shapiro:

> "Why is it that the metaphysically thin, or natureless, or lightweight concept of truth should be a sure-fire sign of expressive and proof-theoretic strength? I suppose that some

deflationists can joyfully accept this situation, saying that metaphysical substance is irrelevant to anything expressive or proof theoretic." [28] page 495.

5
KRIPKE'S THEORY OF TRUTH

5.1 Truth Gaps and Groundedness

We introduced the liar paradox in Chapter 1, and examined various proposals for how it might be resolved. In particular, we examined the language-levels approach of Tarski. This he fully developed into his semantic conception of truth, presented here in Chapter 3. However, Tarski's theory suffers from two major limitations. Firstly, it does not allow a language to contain a truth predicate applicable to its own sentences. Secondly, it leads to an ascending hierarchy of languages $L, L^+, L^{++}, ...,$ each with a truth predicate that applies to sentences of the language immediately below in the hierarchy. Hence, rather than an intuitively plausible univocal notion of truth, we have a hierarchy of truth predicates $Tr_1, Tr_2, Tr_3, \ldots$ In this chapter we examine an alternative approach first suggested by Saul Kripke [19] that avoids both of these limitations.

If a language contains its own truth predicate, then this *cannot* consistently satisfy the *equivalence schema*

$$\text{(ES)} \qquad Tr(<\phi>) \leftrightarrow \phi$$

for all sentences ϕ since by the *diagonal lemma* from 2.2 there is a sentence λ satisfying

$$\lambda \leftrightarrow \neg Tr(<\lambda>)$$

which leads to a contradiction. The theory that Kripke outlined retains (ES) for all sentences *not* involving the truth predicate, and retains the full generality of the conditional from left to right. However the conditional from right to left needs to be restricted in some suitable manner to avoid paradox.

Recall from 1.4 that we might resolve the liar paradox readily by insisting that sentences such as the liar sentence are neither true or false, or that they *lack* a truth value. However, it is not clear how to determine which sentences ought to lack truth value. If this is done merely on the grounds that to assign a truth value would result in paradox, then it is vulnerable to the charge of being entirely *ad hoc*. Another difficulty is that, in view of the strengthened liar paradox, the truth value gap solution might resolve the weakest version of the paradox only to fall to stronger formulations of it. We return to the consideration of the strengthened liar in 5.3.

It might be hoped that those sentences that lead to paradox could be identified by some feature of their syntax. Kripke recognised that this is not the case. In certain circumstances whether or not a set of sentences leads to paradox may depend upon contingent facts, as the following minimal example shows:

S_1 : the planet most distant

from the sun is Neptune.

S_2 : S_3 is false.

S_3 : both S_1 and S_2 are true.

Suppose that S_1 were false. Then immediately S_3 is also false, so that S_2 is true. In this case no paradox arises.

Now suppose that S_1 were true. If S_2 is also true, then S_3 is false and it follows that S_2 is false. If on the other hand S_2 is false, then S_3 is true and it follows that S_2 is true. In either case a contradiction ensues.

Hence in this example whether or not a paradox arises depends upon a contingent fact, namely whether or not there is a planet further away from the sun than Neptune; this is, of course, an open question. As Kripke concludes,

> "It would be fruitless to look for an *intrinsic* criterion that will enable us to sieve out - as meaningless, or ill-formed - those sentences which lead to paradox. The moral: an adequate

theory must allow our statements involving the notion of truth to be *risky*: they risk being paradoxical if the empirical facts are extremely (and unexpectedly) unfavourable. There can be no syntactic or semantic 'sieve' that will winnow out the 'bad' cases while preserving the 'good' ones." [19]

This has not been widely appreciated, with subsequent writers qualifying schemas with disclaimers such as 'avoiding paradoxical instances', as if it were a trivial matter to achieve this. Kripke also observes that it is not only those sentences that lead to paradox that are problematic. Consider the so called *truth-teller* sentence:

this sentence is true

Unlike the liar sentence, which if assumed to be true or to be false produces a contradiction, the truth-teller sentence can be assumed consistently either to be true or to be false. In neither case does a contradiction occur. On attempting to evaluate its truth value, we find that it is true just in case it is true, and so on, in an infinite regress.

Kripke recognised that sentences such as the liar sentence and the truth-teller sentence lack a property that he called *groundedness*, which I now describe. One defines a *truth* predicate and a *falsity* predicate, both of which initially have empty extensions, that is to say they are not satisfied by any sentences. One then considers sentences that include only predicates other than the truth and falsity predicates such as "snow is white" and "grass is blue". According to whether or not the entity named satisfies the predicate, we assign these sentences to the extensions of the truth and falsity predicates respectively. So, assuming that the contingent facts are that snow *is* white but that grass is *not* blue, the first sentence will be assigned to the extension of *true*, and the second to the extension of *false*.

Next, one considers those sentences that satisfy the truth predicate, and those that satisfy the falsity predicate, to generate the sentences

"snow is white" is true

and

"grass is blue" is false.

These too will be assigned to the extension of the truth predicate. In a similar manner, the sentences

"snow is white" is false

and

"grass is blue" is true

will be assigned to the extension of the falsity predicate. Once a given sentence is assigned to the extension either of the truth or the falsity predicate, it remains in that extension. The process is iterated, so that at the next stage

""snow is white" is true" is true

will be assigned to the extension of the truth predicate, and so on. The *grounded* sentences of the language are those that eventually are assigned by this process to the extension of one or the other predicate. The *ungrounded* sentences, of which the liar sentence is an example, will not be assigned to the extension of either predicate at any stage of the process, and consequently lack truth value.

5.2 Formalising Kripke's Theory

We shall make Kripke's suggestion more formal. Suppose that we have a language L containing names $a, b, c, ...$ and non-semantic predicates $F, G, ...$ We construct a sequence of interpretations $I_0, I_1, I_2, ...$ that capture the intuition of successively assigning truth values to more and more of the sentences of L.

The interpretation of the non-semantic predicates will be fixed at I_0 and remain constant through all subsequent interpretations. We define two further predicates, the truth predicate Tr and the falsity predicate Fl. At I_0 both predicates have empty extension.

At the interpretation I_1 we wish to include in the extension of Tr all of those atomic sentences of L where the non-semantic predicate is satisfied, and to include in the extension of Fl all of those atomic sentences of L where the non-semantic predicate is not satisfied. Hence we define

$$I_1(Tr) = \{Fa : a \text{ satisfies } F\}$$

$$I_1(Fl) = \{Fa : a \text{ does not satisfy } F\}$$

At the interpretation I_2 we now wish to include in the extension of Tr and Fl certain sentences that involve single applications of those predicates. We do this as follows:

$$I_2(Tr) = I_1(Tr)$$
$$\cup \{\phi : \phi = Tr(<\phi_1>) \text{ and } \phi_1 \text{ satisfies } Tr\}$$
$$\cup \{\phi : \phi = Fl(<\phi_1>) \text{ and } \phi_1 \text{ satisfies } Fl\}$$

$$I_2(Fl) = I_1(Fl)$$
$$\cup \{\phi : \phi = Tr(<\phi_1>) \text{ and } \phi_1 \text{ satisfies } Fl\}$$
$$\cup \{\phi : \phi = Fl(<\phi_1>) \text{ and } \phi_1 \text{ satisfies } Tr\}$$

I_3 is defined similarly from I_2, I_4 from I_3, and so on. Notice that we do not make any definitions and the basis of sentences *not* belonging to the extensions of Tr and Fl, as this would allow ungrounded sentences to obtain truth values.

Assuming that L is to contain the usual logical connectives, we must extend our definition to include these. We wish a disjunction of sentences to be true when *either* of its disjuncts are true, and to be false when *both* of its disjuncts are false. Hence at each level we require

$$\phi_1 \lor \phi_2 \in I_{n+1}(Tr) \text{ iff } \phi_1 \in I_n(Tr) \text{ or } \phi_2 \in I_n(Tr)$$

$$\phi_1 \lor \phi_2 \in I_{n+1}(Fl) \text{ iff } \phi_1 \in I_n(Fl) \text{ and } \phi_2 \in I_n(Fl).$$

Negation requires more care. It is extremely tempting to suggest that the negation of a sentence ϕ is true whenever ϕ does not belong to the extension of *Tr*. However, since ungrounded sentences fail to belong to the extension of *Tr* this would result in their negations being declared true. This is not what Kripke intended. Rather, the negation of a sentence ϕ is true whenever ϕ belongs to the extension of *Fl*. Hence we require

$$\neg\phi \in I_{n+1}(Tr) \text{ iff } \phi \in I_n(Fl)$$

$$\neg\phi \in I_{n+1}(Fl) \text{ iff } \phi \in I_n(Tr).$$

A subtle consequence of this is that whereas from *outside* L 'not true' means either false or ungrounded, from *inside* L 'not true' means simply false, as would be the case in a theory that did not allow truth gaps. Since these definitions accord with the Strong Kleene three valued logic, for which De Morgan's laws hold, we can treat conjunctions of sentences in the usual way by employing negation and disjunction, avoiding the need to complicate our definition further. Furthermore, as Kripke himself remarks, all of the above can be converted into a definition via *satisfaction* should we wish to cater for a language with quantifiers.

Finally, for ease of reference we recount the definitions of the extensions of Tr and Fl:

$$I_{n+1}(Tr) = I_n(Tr)$$

$\cup \{\phi : \phi = Tr(< \phi_1 >) \text{ and } \phi_1 \text{ satisfies } Tr\}$

$\cup \{\phi : \phi = Fl(< \phi_1 >) \text{ or } \phi = \neg\phi_1 \text{ and } \phi_1 \text{ satisfies } Fl\}$

$\cup \{\phi : \phi = \phi_1 \vee \phi_2 \text{ and }$

at least one of ϕ_1 and ϕ_2 satisfies $Tr\}$

$$I_{n+1}(Fl) = I_n(Fl)$$

$\cup \{\phi : \phi = Tr(< \phi_1 >) \text{ and } \phi_1 \text{ satisfies } Fl\}$

$\cup \{\phi : \phi = Fl(< \phi_1 >) \text{ or } \phi = \neg\phi_1 \text{ and } \phi_1 \text{ satisfies } Tr\}$

$\cup \{\phi : \phi = \phi_1 \vee \phi_2 \text{ and both } \phi_1 \text{ and } \phi_2 \text{ satisfy } Fl\}$.

Example

Consider a language containing the names *snow* and *coal* and the predicate *white* whose extension is just snow, in which we may construct only the following sentences:

S_1 : snow is white

S_2 : coal is white

S_3 : S_1 is true

S_4 : S_2 is false

S_5 : S_5 is false

S_6 : S_4 or S_5

At I_0 the extension of both Tr and Fl are empty. Because *snow* belongs to the extension of *white* but *coal* does not, at I_1 the sentence S_1 is assigned to the extension of Tr, whilst S_2 is assigned to the extension of Fl. At I_2 the sentences S_3 and S_4 will be assigned to the extension of Tr. Finally, at I_3 the sentence S_6 will be assigned to the extension of Tr. In the subsequent interpretations from I_4 onwards, no further sentences are assigned to the extension of either Tr or Fl. In particular, notice that the liar sentence S_5 is not assigned to either extension at any interpretation. The interpretation I_4 is called a *fixed point* for this language. Truth and falsity may be defined by their extensions at the fixed point.

Languages with sentences of arbitrary complexity will not have a fixed point at any finite level of interpretation. However, it is possible to extend the inductive process to transfinite levels (see [20] for introduction to transfinite ordinal numbers) to obtain fixed point interpretations for languages with infinitely many sentences.

5.3 Objections to Kripke's Theory

One of the first difficulties faced by Kripke's theory is how to motivate the idea that certain sentences should lack truth value in the first place. As Kirkham says,

> "He has no independent reasons, other than to
> solve the paradox, for placing the restrictions
> he does on what can and cannot have a truth

value."

Schmitt attempts to motivate truth gaps using an example of *vagueness*. Where a property is vague, in the sense of allowing borderline cases, he claims that sentences may be produced that are neither true nor false:

> "If Joe has a borderline case of baldness, then 'Joe is bald' is neither true nor false, even though it may still be the case that either Joe is bald or he is not bald."

This surely is mistaken. The sentence 'Joe is bald' is true just in case Joe *is* bald, and is false just in case he is *not* bald. For the sentence to be neither true nor false, it would have to be that Joe was neither bald nor not bald. Now it is one thing to claim that the *semantic* law of excluded middle admits exceptions, but quite another to claim the same for the *logical* law of excluded middle, namely that any entity be *P* or *not P*. Surely the difficulty is that in the situation no adequate criteria of *baldness* has been established against which to decide whether Joe is bald or not. The fact that in a borderline case one would not wish to commit oneself to a *judgement* as to whether x is P or not, does not alter the logical fact that in any situation x must be P or *not* P, once a clear prescription of what it is to be P has been given.

Next, we note the peculiarity that in Kripke's solution it is only the *truth* predicate that admits objects, in particular sentences, that neither satisfy nor does not satisfy it. If, contrary to the claim of deflationists, truth defines a genuine predicate, then it should not be treated any differently from other predicates. So the question arises, can we motivate the idea that most or even all predicates have objects that neither satisfy them nor do not satisfy them.

Perhaps it is for this reason that some have tried to motivate predicate gaps via the notion of *category errors*. Consider for example the number *three* and the predicate corresponding to the property of *redness*. Now clearly we would not wish to assert that *three is red*. But would be wish to assert that *three is not red?* Is it not more accurate to say that *three* falls outside of the domain to which *redness* applies. Perhaps a similar phenomenon is occurs with the *truth* predicate, in that certain sentences fall outside of the domain of those things to which the predicate can be said to apply. However, this is not entirely convincing as the liar sentence is, by definition, a sentence. So it ought to belong to the domain to which the truth predicate properly applies. Tyler Burge notes this difficulty:

> "Paradoxical statements can be constructed in which the reference of the singular term seems to be the right *sort* of thing for the semantical predicate to apply to - for almost any independently motivated view as to what the right sort is. The relevance of category considerations is thus obscure." [ ] p.86.

In conclusion, there does not appear to be any satisfactory way of motivating the truth gap approach.

5.4 The Strengthened Liar Paradox Revisited

Suppose that S is an ungrounded sentence in our language L, so that S does not receive a truth value at the fixed point interpretation. We might wonder about the truth values of the following sentences:

S is true S is false

Since S does not receive a truth value it is neither true nor false, so that it is not true and not false. Hence at first sight our intuition may be that the two sentences above are false. Indeed, this opinion is widely held. For example, Susan Haack writes:

> "Suppose 'p' to be neither true nor false; then the left hand side of:
>
> 'p' is true iff p
>
> will be, presumably, false, while to right hand side will be neither true nor false." [14] page 101.

More recently Frederick Schmitt makes almost the same point:

> "'p' has *no truth value*, but the left hand side, ' $<p>$ is true', has the value *false*, since it is false that $<p>$ is true (because $<p>$ has no truth value)." [27] page 136.

> "It is hard to see how 'p' could have

indeterminate truth-value while '$< p >$ is true' also has indeterminate truth-value. If 'p' has indeterminate truth-value, then it is not merely not true but downright false that $< p >$ has the value true. So '$< p >$ is true' is false." [27] page 137.

These claims are incorrect, at least for Kripke's theory. Unfortunately both writers proceed to use these claims to support further incorrect conclusions. Haack argues that Convention T entails bivalence and thus rules out theories that make use of truth gaps. Schmitt makes almost the same point, arguing that deflationism (in the minimalist sense that truth is constituted merely by the totality of T-sentences) entails bivalence. Since he regards non-bivalent theories to be adequately motivated by examples of vagueness, he uses the contrapositive that non-bivalence entails non-deflationism in an attempted rebuttal of deflationism.

Some reflection upon the inductive method of obtaining successive interpretations of Tr and Fl described in 5.2 reveals that if ϕ is an ungrounded sentence, then so are $Tr(<\phi>)$ and $Fl(<\phi>)$. If, for example, $Tr(<\phi>)$ had received a truth value at interpretation I_n, then ϕ itself must have received a truth value at I_{n-1}. But this cannot be the case since ϕ is ungrounded. It follows that we can never apply the Tr and Fl predicates to a sentence that lacks truth value and thereby obtain a new sentence that has a truth value. Kripke is quite specific on this point, stating

> "$Tr(<\phi>)$ is to be true, or false, respectively iff ϕ is true or false. It follows that $Tr(<\phi>)$ suffers a truth gap if ϕ does." [19] (notation modified)

These considerations impact upon whether or not Kripke's theory resolves the strengthened liar paradox. The answer is not clear cut since there are a multitude of versions of the strengthened liar. The most usual formulation is the sentence

$$(\lambda_S)\ \lambda_S \text{ is not true}$$

Taking this formulation, Kirkham argues that the paradox is *not* resolved by Kripke's theory. I believe that he is mistaken, having fallen victim to the same misconception as Haack and Schmitt. Since the strengthened liar sentence is ungrounded it will not receive at truth value under any of the interpretations, that is to say it will be neither true nor false. Kirkham argues thus:

> "If it is neither true nor false (and thus *not true*), then it is precisely what it claims to be, so it is true." [18] page 293, italics mine.

The misconception once again is that although λ_S is not true from the perspective of *outside* the language, because it is ungrounded, we cannot conclude *within* the language that 'λ_S is not true' is true. Kripke makes this point himself:

> "A typically ungrounded sentence such as
>
> (3)   (3) is true
>
> will, of course, receive no truth value in the process just sketched. In particular, it will never be called 'true'. But the subject cannot express this fact by saying, '(3) is not true.' Such an assertion would conflict directly with

the stipulation that he should deny that a sentence is true precisely under the circumstances under which he would deny the sentence itself." [19].

"Liar sentences are *not true* in the object language, in the sense that the inductive process never makes them true; but we are precluded from saying this in the object language by our interpretation of negation and the truth predicate." [19]

It follows that no contradiction arises from allowing that λ_S be neither true nor false so that Kripke's theory *does* resolve this version of the strengthened liar.

We may explore these issues further. Supposing that ϕ is an ungrounded sentence, we have already argued that $Tr(<\phi>)$ and $Fl(<\phi>)$ must also be ungrounded. It follows that

$$Tr(<\phi>) \lor Fl(<\phi>) \text{ and } \neg(Tr(<\phi>) \lor Fl(<\phi>))$$

are also ungrounded. But the latter statement asserts that ϕ is neither true nor false, which is precisely the property that ϕ has by virtue of being ungrounded. We might expect, looking from the outside, this to be true. Our conclusion that within L it is neither true nor false shows that L cannot 'recognise' its ungrounded sentences as being such. Groundedness is a concept that, if it is to be expressed at all, must be expressed in a metalangauge. As Kripke remarks

> "Such semantical notions as 'grounded,' 'paradoxical,' etc. belong to the metalanguage. This situation seems to me to be intuitively acceptable; in contrast to the notion of truth, none of these notions is to be found in natural language in its pristine purity, before philosophers reflect on its semantics (in particular, the semantic paradoxes). " [19]

We can of course still formulate the strengthened liar in the metalanguage thus:

this sentence is false or ungrounded

But in Kripke's theory this is not a sentence of the object language, so that the paradox cannot arise in the object language.

Kripke does not give formal axioms for his theory, but such axioms were proposed by Solomon Feferman in [8], and have come to be known as *KF*. In particular, these satisfy 'half' of Convention T, namely for each sentence ϕ

$$KF \vdash Tr(\lceil \phi \rceil) \rightarrow \phi.$$

Furthermore, Kripke claims that

> "all the truth predicates of the finite Tarski hierarchy are definable within [the fixed point language], and all the languages of that hierarchy are sub-languages of [the fixed point language]." [19]

This fact is encompassed by Feferman's axioms, so that *KF* in a sense contains *TS*. Consequently, we also have

$$PA \cup KF \vdash (\forall x)(prov(x) \rightarrow Tr(x))$$

so that the non-conservativeness results demonstrated by Ketland for *TS* may be matched by similar results for *KF*. Indeed, *KF* greatly surpasses *TS* in deductive power because we also have

$$PA \cup KF \vdash G^*$$

where G^* is the Gödel sentence for $PA \cup TS$. In fact KF can also derive the Gödel sentence for the meta-metatheory $(PA \cup TS) \cup TS'$, where TS' is Tarski's theory applied to sentences of L^+, and so on for many iterations. This suggests that Kripke's theory provides a viable alternative to the Tarskian approach.

However, Kripke's theory is not without its own drawbacks. For example, since the liar sentence λ lacks truth value, so does

$$Tr(\ulcorner \lambda \urcorner) \rightarrow Tr(\ulcorner \lambda \urcorner).$$

Consequently, we are unable to obtain generalisations such as

$$(\forall x)(Tr(x) \rightarrow Tr(x))$$

which is the intuitively reasonable assertion that every true sentence is true. Such difficulties are addressed by the rule-of-revision semantics proposed variously by Gupta, Herzberger, and Belnap [22]. Unfortunately, there is not space to take up these issues here.

REFERENCES

[1] J. L. Austin, *Truth*, Aristotelian Society, supplementary volume 24 (1950), page references to reprint in [3]

[2] Simon Blackburn, *Spreading the Word*, OUP (1984).

[3] Simon Blackburn and Keith Simmons (editors), *Truth*, OUP (1999).

[4] George S. Boolos and Richard C. Jeffrey, *Computability and Logic*, CUP (1974).

[5] Donald Davidson, *The Folly of Trying to Define Truth*, Journal of Philosophy, volume 93 (1996), page references to reprint in [3].

[6] Julian Dodd, *An Identity Theory of Truth*, MacMillan (2000).

[7] Solomon Feferman, *Towards Useful Type-Free Theories, I,* originally in Journal of Symbolic Logic (1982), reprinted in [22]

[8] Solomon Feferman, *Reflecting on Incompleteness*, Journal of Symbolic Logic (1991).

[9] Hartry Field, *Deflationist Views of Meaning and Content*, Mind 103 (1994), page references to reprint in [3]

[10]Hartry Field, *Deflating the Conservativeness Argument*, Journal of Philosophy, volume 96 (1999)

[11]Gottlob Frege, *The Basic Laws of Arithmetic*, originally 1902, University of California (1964)

[12]D. A. Gillies, *Frege, Dedekind and Peano on the Foundations of Arithmetic*, Van Gorcum (1982).

[13]Kurt Gödel, *On Formally Undecidable Propositions in Principia Mathematica and Related Systems*, Monatshefte für Mathematic und Physik, volume 38 (1931).

[14]Susan Haack, *Philosophy of Logics*, CUP (1978).

[15]Paul Horwich, *Truth*, Blackwell (1990).

[16]Jeffrey Ketland, *Deflationism and Tarski's Paradise*, Mind 108 (1999).

[17]Jeffrey Ketland, *A Proof of the (Strengthened) Liar Sentence*, Analysis (2000).

[18]Richard L. Kirkham, *Theories of Truth*, MIT (1992).

[19]Saul Kripke, *Outline of a Theory of Truth*, Journal of Philosophy, volume 72 (1975), reprinted in [22].

[20]E. J. Lemmon, *Introduction to Axiomatic Set Theory*, Routledge & Kegan Paul (1968).

[21]Leonard Linsky (editor), *Semantics and the Philosophy of Language*, University of Illinois (1952).

[22]Robert L. Martin, *Recent Essays on Truth and the Liar Paradox*, OUP (1984).

[23]Roger Penrose, *The Emperor's New Mind*, OUP (1989).

[24]Willard V. Quine, *Philosophy of Logic*, Harvard University Press (1970).

[25]Frank P. Ramsey, *On Facts and Propositions*,

Proceedings of the Aristotelian Society, supplementary volume 7, extract reprinted in [3].

[26]Bertrand Russell, *The Problems of Philosophy*, OUP (1912).

[27]Frederick Schmitt, *Truth: A Primer*, Westview Press (1995)

[28]Stewart Shapiro, *Proof and Truth: Through Thick and Thin*, Journal of Philosophy, volume 95 (1998).

[29]Alfred Tarski, *The Concept of Truth in Formalised Languages*, Polish original published in Warsaw (1933), English translation with postscript reprinted in [33]

[30]Alfred Tarski, *The Establishment of Scientific Semantics*, originally in Przeglad Filozoficzny, volume 39 (1936), reprinted in [33].

[31]Alfred Tarski, *The Semantic Conception of Truth and the Foundations of Semantics*, originally in Philosophy and Phenomenological Research volume 4 (1944) reprinted in [21].

[32]Alfred Tarski, *Truth and Proof*, Scientific American

220 (June 1969).

[33]Alfred Tarski, *Logic, Semantics, Metamathematics*, OUP (1956).

[34]Crispin Wright, *Truth: A Traditional Debate Reviewed*, Canadian Journal of Philosophy, supplementary volume 24 (1999), reprinted in [3].

APPENDIX: PEANO ARITHMETIC AND ROBINSON ARITHMETIC

The theory of *Peano arithmetic*, *PA*, may be expressed in the language of first order predicate calculus equipped with a name **0**, a one-place function name *f*, a pair of two-place function names $+$ and $\cdot$, the two-place predicate symbol $=$, and the usual logical connectives, variables and quantifiers.

The *standard interpretation* has the set of natural numbers $\{0, 1, 2, 3, ...\}$ as its domain. The name **0** is interpreted as the natural number 0. The function name *f* is interpreted as the *successor function*, mapping each natural number *n* to $n + 1$. We define a name for each natural number as follows:

$$1 = f(0), \quad 2 = f(f(0)), \quad 3 = f(f(f(0))), \quad \text{and so on.}$$

The two place functions $+$ and $\cdot$ are interpreted as addition and multiplication respectively, and $=$ is the two-place predicate of identity. To prevent the notation from becoming cumbersome we write x' for $f(x)$. For example, $3 = 0'''$.

The axioms of PA are as follows:

(P1) $\quad (\forall x)(\forall y)(x' = y' \rightarrow x = y)$

(P2) $\quad (\forall x)\neg(x' = 0)$

(P3) $\quad (F0 \wedge (\forall x)(Fx \rightarrow Fx')) \rightarrow (\forall x)Fx$
$\quad\quad\quad$ where F is any predicate.

(P4) $\quad (\forall x)(x + 0 = x)$

(P5) $\quad (\forall x)(\forall y)(x + y' = (x + y)')$

(P6) $\quad (\forall x)(x \cdot 0 = 0)$

(P7) $\quad (\forall x)(\forall y)(x \cdot y' = x \cdot y + x)$

Intuitively, axiom (P1) says that two numbers that have the same successor must be equal. Note that by contraposition, it follows that if two numbers are distinct then their successors are also distinct.

Axiom (P2) says that **0** is not the successor of any number. Rather than being a single axiom, (P3) is an *axiom schema*. (P3) yields one axiom for each predicate *F* that may be formulated in the language of *PA*. Intuitively, it says that if **0** satisfies a particular predicate *F*, and that if the successor of any number satisfying *F* also satisfies *F*, then *all* numbers satisfy *F*. This is known as *mathematical induction*. (P4) and (P5) recursively define the function named + and (P6) and (P7) recursively define the functions named ·

To simplify notation, we drop the distinction between the natural number *n* and the name **n** that is to be interpreted as *n*.

Axioms (P4) and (P5) allow us to prove elementary facts about addition, for example

$$3 + 2 = 3 + 1' = (3 + 1)' = (3 + 0')'$$
$$= (3 + 0)'' = 3'' = 5$$

Axioms (P6) and (P7) allow us to prove elementary facts about multiplication, for example

$$3 \cdot 2 = 3 \cdot 1' = 3 \cdot 1 + 3$$
$$= 3 \cdot 0' + 3 = 3 \cdot 0 + 3 + 3$$
$$= 0 + 3 + 3 = 6$$

As an example of the application of the induction schema, we prove that every number is distinct from its successor, that is:

Theorem $(\forall x)\neg(x = x')$

Proof: Let Fx be $\neg(x = x')$.

Taking x as 0 in (P2) we have $\neg(0 = 0')$, so that we have established $F0$. We call this the *basis* of the induction.

If we have Fx, that is $\neg(x = x')$, then by (P1) we have $\neg(x' = x'')$, so that we have established Fx'. We call this *the inductive step.*   ∎

We prove a complementary result to (P4):

(P4') $(\forall x)(0 + x = x)$

Proof: *Basis:*   By (P4), $0 + 0 = 0$.

Inductive step: If $0 + x = x$, then by (P5) $0 + x' = (0 + x)' = x'$.

Next, we prove a complementary result to (P5):

(P5') $(\forall x)(\forall y)(x' + y = (x+y)')$

Proof: We use induction on *y*.

Basis: By (P4) $x' + 0 = x' = (x+0)'$.

Inductive step: If $x' + y = (x+y)'$ then by (P5)

$x' + y' = (x'+y)' = (x+y)'' = (x+y')'$. ■

We are now ready to prove:

Commutativity of addition:

$$(\forall x)(\forall y)(x+y = y+x)$$

Proof: Again, we use induction on *y*:

Basis: By (P4) and (P4') $x+0 = 0 = 0+x$

Inductive Step: If $x+y = y+x$ then by (P5) and (P5')

$x+y' = (x+y)' = (y+x)' = y'+x$. ■

Associativity of addition:

$$(\forall x)(\forall y)(\forall z)((x+y)+z = x+(y+z))$$

Proof: We use induction on z:

Basis: By (P4) $(x+y)+0 = x+y = x+(y+0)$

Inductive Step: If $(x+y)+z = x+(y+z)$ then by (P5)

$$(x+y)+z' = ((x+y)+z)' = (x+(y+z))'$$
$$= x+(y+z)' = x+(y+z')$$

∎

Moving on to multiplication, we prove first that:

1 is the unity: $(\forall x)(x \cdot 1 = x)$

Proof: By (P7), (P6) and (P4')

$$x \cdot 1 = x \cdot 0' = x \cdot 0 + x = 0 + x = x.$$ ∎

We may prove a complementary result to (P6):

(P6') $(\forall x)(0 \cdot x = 0)$

Proof: *Basis:* By (P6) $0 \cdot 0 = 0$

Inductive Step: If $0 \cdot x = 0$ then by (P7) and (P4)

$$0 \cdot x' = 0 \cdot x + 0 = 0 + 0 = 0.$$ ∎

We also have a complementary result to (P7):

(P7') $(\forall x)(\forall y)(x' \cdot y = x \cdot y + y)$

Proof: We use induction on y:

Basis: By (P6) and (P4) $x' \cdot 0 = 0 = 0 + 0 = x \cdot 0 + 0$

Inductive step: If $x' \cdot y = x \cdot y + y$ then by (P7) and (P5)

$$x' \cdot y' = x' \cdot y + x' = x \cdot y + y + x' = (x \cdot y + y + x)'$$
$$= (x \cdot y + x + y)' = x \cdot y + x + y' = x \cdot y' + y'$$

∎

We are now ready to prove:

Commutativity of multiplication:

$$(\forall x)(\forall y)(x \cdot y = y \cdot x)$$

Proof: We use induction on y:

Basis: By (P6) and (P6') $x \cdot 0 = 0 = 0 \cdot x$

Inductive step: If $x \cdot y = y \cdot x$ then by (P7) and (P7')

$$x \cdot y' = x \cdot y + x = y \cdot x + x = y' \cdot x$$ ∎

Distributive law:

$$(\forall x)(\forall y)(\forall z)(x \cdot (y + z) = x \cdot y + x \cdot z)$$

Proof: We use induction on x:

Basis: By (P6') and (P4)

$$0 \cdot (y + z) = 0 = 0 + 0 = 0 \cdot y + 0 \cdot z$$

Inductive step: If $x \cdot (y + z) = x \cdot y + x \cdot z$ then by (P7')

$$x' \cdot (y+z) = x \cdot (y+z) + y + z$$
$$= x \cdot y + x \cdot z + y + z$$
$$= (x \cdot y + y) + (x \cdot z + z)$$
$$= x' \cdot y + x' \cdot z$$

■

Associativity of multiplication:

$$(\forall x)(\forall y)(\forall z)((x \cdot y) \cdot z = x \cdot (y \cdot z))$$

Proof: We use induction on z:

Basis: By (P6) $(x \cdot y) \cdot 0 = 0 = x \cdot 0 = x \cdot (y \cdot 0)$

Inductive step: If $(x \cdot y) \cdot z = x \cdot (y \cdot z)$ then by (P7) and the distributive law:

$$(x \cdot y) \cdot z' = (x \cdot y) \cdot z + x \cdot y$$
$$= x \cdot (y \cdot z) + x \cdot y$$
$$= x \cdot (y \cdot z + y)$$
$$= x \cdot (y \cdot z')$$

■

Robinson arithmetic Q lacks the induction schema
(P3) of PA, and in its place has

$$(\forall x)(x = \mathbf{0} \vee (\exists y)(x = y')).$$

Intuitively, this says that apart from 0 every number is
the successor of some number. Notice that this
axiom follows from (P3) by taking Fx to be
$x = \mathbf{0} \vee (\exists y)(x = y')$, and hence all theorems of Q are
also theorems of PA.

However Q is *much* weaker than PA. Q is able to
prove individual cases of arithmetic laws but not their
generalisations, for example

$$Q \vdash 5 + 7 = 7 + 5 \text{ but } not$$

$$Q \vdash (\forall x)(\forall y)(x + y = y + x)$$

Q is interesting because it is finitely axiomatised and,
despite being much weaker than PA, Gödel's
incompleteness theorems are still applicable.

www.ingramcontent.com/pod-product-compliance
Lightning Source LLC
Chambersburg PA
CBHW052106090426
42741CB00009B/1696